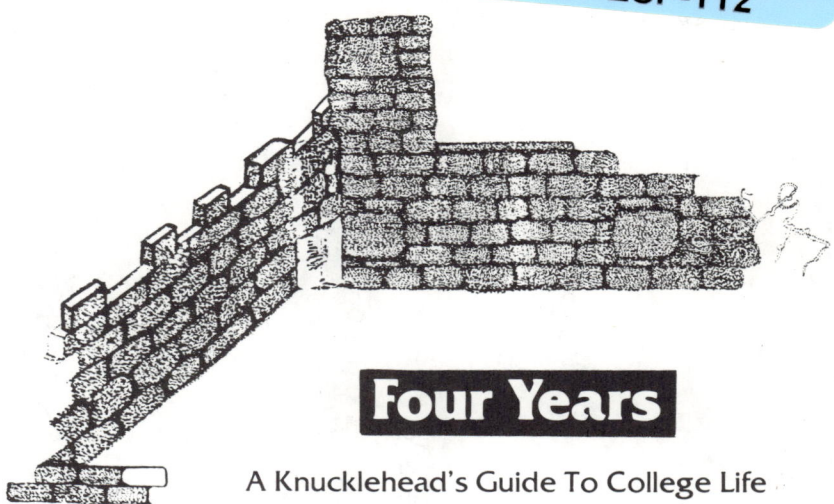

Four Years

A Knucklehead's Guide To College Life

*the incubation of thoughts
and the hatching of ideas...*

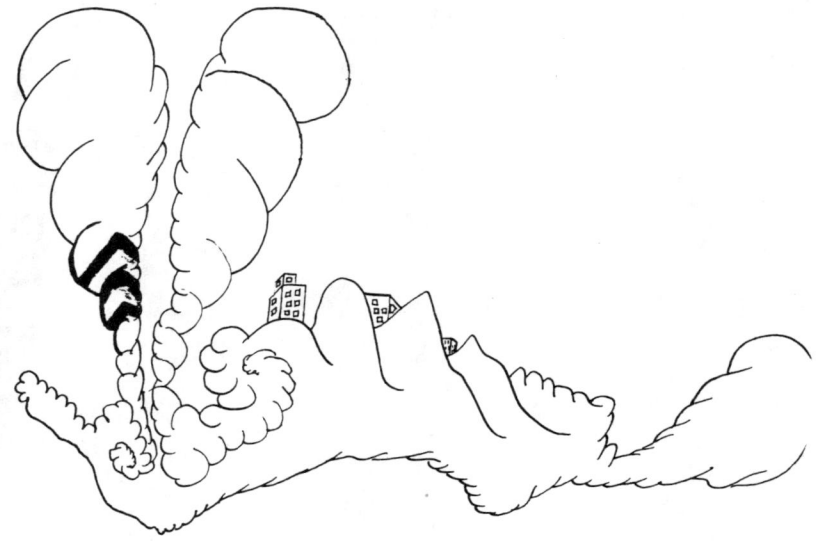

To Wayne
   you are the eyes of the world...

and John
　　　you are the ears...

and Jim
 you are the mouth.

and friends

With the falling of the leaves, the masks of green are stripped off the hillsides, revealing the diversity and uniqueness of each ridge and valley hitherto unseen. It is in the winter, when the hills bare their innermost selves, that we get to know them. Then, in the spring, when the masks return, we can look at the hills as old friends few others understand.

—JW

Four Years

A Knucklehead's Guide To College Life

To College Life A Knucklehead's Guide

KNUT HOUSE

Tar Beach
Phailand

Suffragette City
Beannyville

Four Years

Copyright 1988 by Knuthouse. All rights reserved.
Printed in the United States of America
Information, comments, complaints, questions, additional
copies ($6.95) or just to be friendly address:
                KNUT HOUSE
                215 Godwin Ave.
                Tower C
            Midland Park, NJ 07432

All letters answered (SASE appreciated)

NJ residents please add .42 sales tax per copy

LIBRARY OF CONGRESS
CATALOG CARD NUMBER:

88-82195

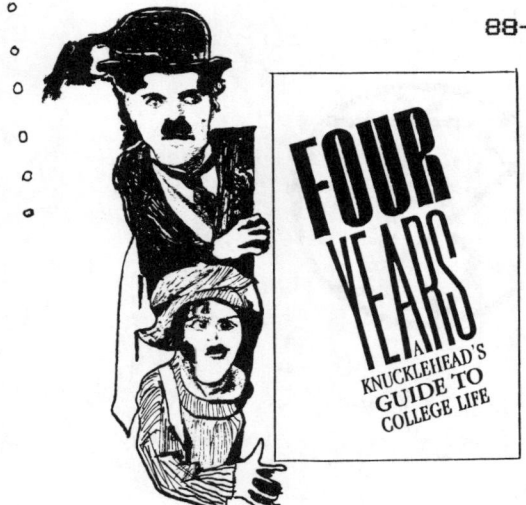

ISBN 0-9620414-0-8

Four Years

I. Foreyears...
II. Who The Hell Am I?
III. Who The Hell Are You?
IV. Before...
V. What Am I Doing Here?
VI. Friends
VII. Work!
VIII. Professors: Surprisingly Human
IX. Who's In Charge Here?
X. Friends (Again)
XI. Bless This Mess
XII. Fraternities
XIII. Sororities
XIV. Sports
XV. Recreation
XVI. Sex...
XVII. Drugs...
XVIII. And Rock & Roll
XIX. Beating The System
XX. Door Prizes
XXI. After...

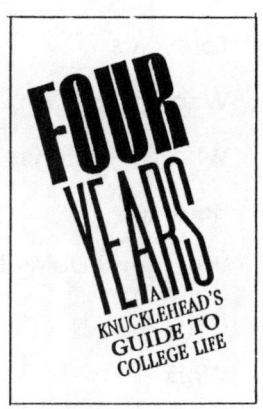

opinion 1: a belief stronger than impression and less strong than positive knowledge 2: JUDGEMENT 3: a formal statement by an expert after careful study

I.
Foreyears...

For years I've wanted to write a book like this. A short, readable, thoroughly candid guide for the college bound student. A collection of experiences, insights, memories and advice that will paint the scene, hopefully answer some questions, and at the very least earn me three credits in English almost effortlessly. A spine tingling, non-stop page turner; a stupendous thriller that pulses with unbridled excitement. A block buster of a...well, maybe not. A kind of factual handbook that you might actually find as enjoyable as it is useful. The Chinese fortune cookie of College.

A book like this could very easily read like a textbook. I could write it in about three days if I wanted it to sound like one. The bulk of my labor stems from a desire to come up with something that is both informative and entertaining. I hope you appreciate the extra effort.

Throughout college I had the good fortune of being surrounded by some of the classic characters of our time. Never before has such a colorful grouping of personalities been assembled and each one contributes in some way to this work. But even though you're getting a pretty diverse account here, I still wouldn't want you to take everything said as Gospel. A popular student misconception is that the written page signifies the truth, the whole truth, etc. Not so. Personal viewpoints creep into everything—College textbooks, articles, short, readable handbooks, essays. Look for opinions and slanted statements—they will be all over what you'll be reading in the next four years. Question these. College has a lot to do with questioning. Once in a while it provides some answers.

It is easy in the world to live after the world's opinion; it is easy in solitude to live after our own; but the great man is he who in the midst of the crowd keeps with perfect sweetness the independence of solitude.

—RWE

By pursuing his own interest an idividual frequently promotes that of the society more effectually than when he really intends to promote it.

—AS

Isn't this the life—to be young, stupid, and have no future.

—DU

We want you alive for the sequel.

To order:
Send $6.95

+

2. shipping

to

KNUTHOUSE
215 GODWIN AVENUE
DEPT. 254
MIDLAND PARK, NJ 07432

For the next four years you'll have
excitement, challenges, acheivement,
recognition, exploration, discovery,
innovation, inspiration, fantasy, pr⟨
fascination, animation, laughs, exhi⟨
controversy, responsibility, apprecia
satisfaction, stimulation, suspense,
melodrama, amusement, merriment, fri⟨
books, magazines, newspapers, announ⟨
bright people, cool people, funny pe⟨
wise people, creative people, intima⟨
comraderie, mentors, counselors, advi
contacts, football games, video games
basketball courts, weights, ping pong
frisbee wars, pinball, pool, poker ga
backgammon, guts, vending machines, s
popcorn, cheeseburgers, pizza, ice cr
running water, peanut butter and jell
programs, organizations, music, art,
theatre, movies, concerts, motown, al
attention, attraction, hawking opport
snowball fights, funnelating, soul br
Christmas trees, barbecues, re-runs,
poison ivy, investment peas, rags & b
paper clips, rubber bands, copy machi
postage stamps, nose tape, phone boot
toilet paper, light bulbs, garbage di
fire extinguishers, the yellow pages,
right at your fingertips.

> Why would you even think about
> getting into a car and driving
> anywhere drunk.

**DYING YOUNG IS THE WORST TRAGEDY
THERE IS.**

II.
Who The Hell Am I?

I'm a creative thinker, an imaginative, somewhat brilliant writer and a semi-professional airhead. I enjoy being entertained and watch almost everything with low-key amusement. I gave up being a cynic years ago in favor of being a calculated space cadet. I've made an art form of dizziness. Most people that know me seem to like me. Most people that don't know me tolerate me. I hate making waves and I trip going up stairs sometimes.

I learn from everything and am an intent observer. sometimes go for days without saying five complete sentences but I love to put thoughts on paper. Somehow words seem more lasting that way. I've been gifted with some sort of special connection between my eyes and hands that allows me to translate what I see onto paper almost effortlessly, but that somehow doesn't carry over to such simple tasks as sharpening pencils and opening doors.

I am by no means a stylistically or technically proficient writer and I have a crummy vocabulary by most author's standards. I like to think I make up for it in sarcasm, understatement and ambiguity.

The world is still a pretty nice place despite some of the things we've done to it; people are still its greatest asset. I see good traits in people rather easily and tend to forget about the lousy ones as easily. I've stopped trying to see through everybody and now concentrate on seeing through everything else. I'm your basic laid-back sort of character.[1] I want to be remembered for not sticking out.

I don't always think in complete thoughts and I'm constantly fearful that I've been given too many gears upstairs. The price I pay for being a creative genius[2] is an attention span of about six seconds. For better or worse, I've got a severely hyperactive mind—I can contemplate supply-side economics, Clapton guitar solos, little kids, the Mets and mushrooms in the same breath.

But somehow the important stuff manages to sink in and stick—I remember the events of my stay at college in much the same uncanny way that a squirrel always remembers where he buries his nuts regardless of how long it's been since he's stashed them. I call things like I see things, I'm not especially opinionated, I go off on non-sensical tangents a lot, I disapprove of writers using inane squirrel analogies out of context, I wonder what happened to shows like the Odd Couple, Barney Miller or Columbo.

I wrote this book because I loved college and enjoy writing. If you read it you'll more than likely get a lot out of it. I wish I had a book like this when I was entering college. But make no mistake about my primary intention. Above all else, I'm after author royalties.

[1]Sorry, Bruce
[2]self-proclaimed

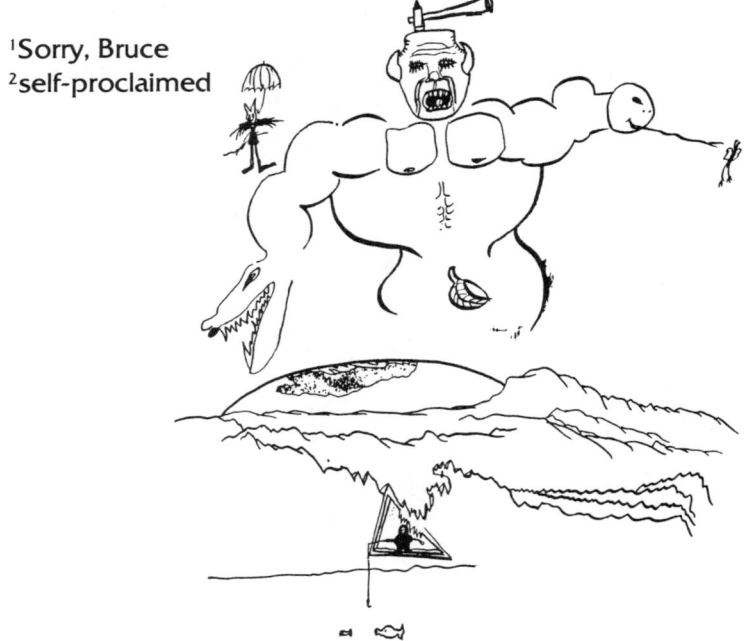

What is easy is seldom excellent

—SJ

III.
Who The Hell Are You?

You are one of several million scholars who have decided to embark on the strange, fantastic, enlightening journey known as higher education. Right now you're a big highschool senior—You're pretty hot stuff; you've got everything all figured out; life's good at the top. Your biggest worries are finding wheels, parties, prom dates. You've already found yourself.

Mom does your laundry, you eat three squares a day, homework is generally useless, two o'clock is a late night. You lead a normal if not slightly mechanized life—you wake up everyday at "x" o'clock; you get home every night at "y" o'clock. You go to school because you're supposed to; you read most books because you have to; you make your bed because you ought to. Your biggest choice is jeans or cords; your biggest responsibility is cleaning your room.

You are governed by an unwritten set of rules that promises red marks for missed assignments, zoo for cutting classes, substantial penalty for early withdrawal., and decapitation for coming home wrecked. You'd like more individuality; you'd love more freedom; you'd die for a few more hours sleep on Sunday mornings. Have I got a deal for you.

This intelligence-testing business reminds me of the way they used to weigh hogs in Texas. They would get a long plank, put it over a cross-bar and somehow tie the hog on one end of the plank. They'd search all around till they found a stone that would balance the weight of the hog and they'd put that on the other end of the plank. Then they'd guess the weight of the stone.

—JD

What do you mean, expense money?

—FS

I'd rather leave while I'm in love.

—RC

IV.
Before...

This isn't a 'Don't forget your toothbrush' chapter. No matter how well you plan, you're still going to leave stuff home and run out of underwear and money in about a week. It doesn't make much sense for me to make this a shopping list of things to do and bring. Do yourself a favor and enjoy your summer; Bring an open mind, some clues, and several thousand in small bills. You'll get by without the other stuff till your next trip home.

I'm assuming that you've been checking into schools, that you have some general information about them, and are at least in the process of deciding where you might like to go. An on-campus visit and interview is a common method of scoping colleges that you're really interested in: You get a personal meeting with a bonafide college representative, possibly a guided tour, and a thoroughly professional sales pitch. What you have to remember about these deals is that you're essentially being sold on a product—the good points will be emphasized and the bad ones will be downplayed if touched on at all. I hope that you'll ask a lot of questions, but that you'll use this information as just a portion of your overall evaluation.

Do some homework on your own. Bring a change of clothes, get out of your formal attire after your interview, and try not to bumble around campus gawking at everything like a tourist from a foreign country. The only reason I'm advising this is that you'll get a much more accurate picture if the established crew can't tell that you're a Pre-Freshman.[1] This might not happen all over, but I know a bunch of guys who used to put on great shows for prospective freshmen and orientation groups. Wild gorillas swinging from trees, being pelted with water balloons, and other assorted acts of questionable taste may adversely color your impression of the college.

The "Large-vs.-Small?" dilemma is a matter of personal preference. Both have their advantages and drawbacks: Large schools offer a wider selection of courses and a more diverse student body, if you don't mind hitch-hiking to classes[2] and feeling kind of insignificant at times. Small schools offer more personal attention and a somewhat more unified student body, if you don't mind seeing many of the same faces daily and having alot of activity monitored by the rest of the campus.

Deciding on a college may or may not be a big deal for you Personally, I didn't give it a whole lot of thought and I happened to luck out. I like to think I'm a rarity though. Ideally, you should go to the best school you get accepted to—even if this means a few lean years on the financial statement.[3]

And "best" is best for you—not "best" by some catalog's criteria or your friend's older sister's boyfriend's standards. Look beyond the obvious. Academics are important and are typically a major consideration in deciding on a college. But you won't absorb a thing if you're miserable in your environment. And you'll never reach your full potential if you don't have the opportunity to explore and excel in other areas. College will be your home for the next four years. Find out about all aspects of it and make your choice as if your life depended on it.[4]

This aside, soak up your friends, your lover, and the sun for all they're worth—things ain't gonna be quite the same when September arrives and as time goes on. Your experiences in the next four years will be among the most intense you'll ever have. You can't help but change and your previous relationships inevitably do the same. The hinges of highschool friendships that you thought would never rust, slowly become eroded by distance and a new set of chumps. This isn't a hard and fast rule, but something that occurs if you choose to do nothing about it. You'll see more and more people less and less[5] and the old friends you do see will be somewhat detached from your new world. They will have moved on—as you have—and maintaining your highschool ties will require a little extra effort when you're back home. Writing letters kind of fizzles out after a semester—two, tops.

Any romantically linked couple that can pull a high-school relationship through college without limiting their own individual experiences has my instant admiration and envy and I would be interested in finding out how they do it. Write me at Knut House—215 Godwin Avenue, Tower C, Midland Park, New Jersey 07432.

[1] Three piece suits, penny loafers, Mom and Pop and necks on springs are dead giveaways

[2] Sarcasm, folks

[3] Practically, this isn't always possible as tuition rates at quality schools are at astronomical levels. Scholarships, loans and grants are available and are worth the extra effort it takes to obtain them. Check with your guidance counselor, your local bank and the college's financial aid office if money is the one thing that is keeping you outside of a particular college's gates.

[4] I didn't want this to sound quite so strong and I considered changing the wording, but if you stop to think about it, it's really sort of profound.

[5] Till finally you see everybody never?

Sometimes it's better to travel in hope than to arrive.
—RLS

Never eat anything with a face.
—JV

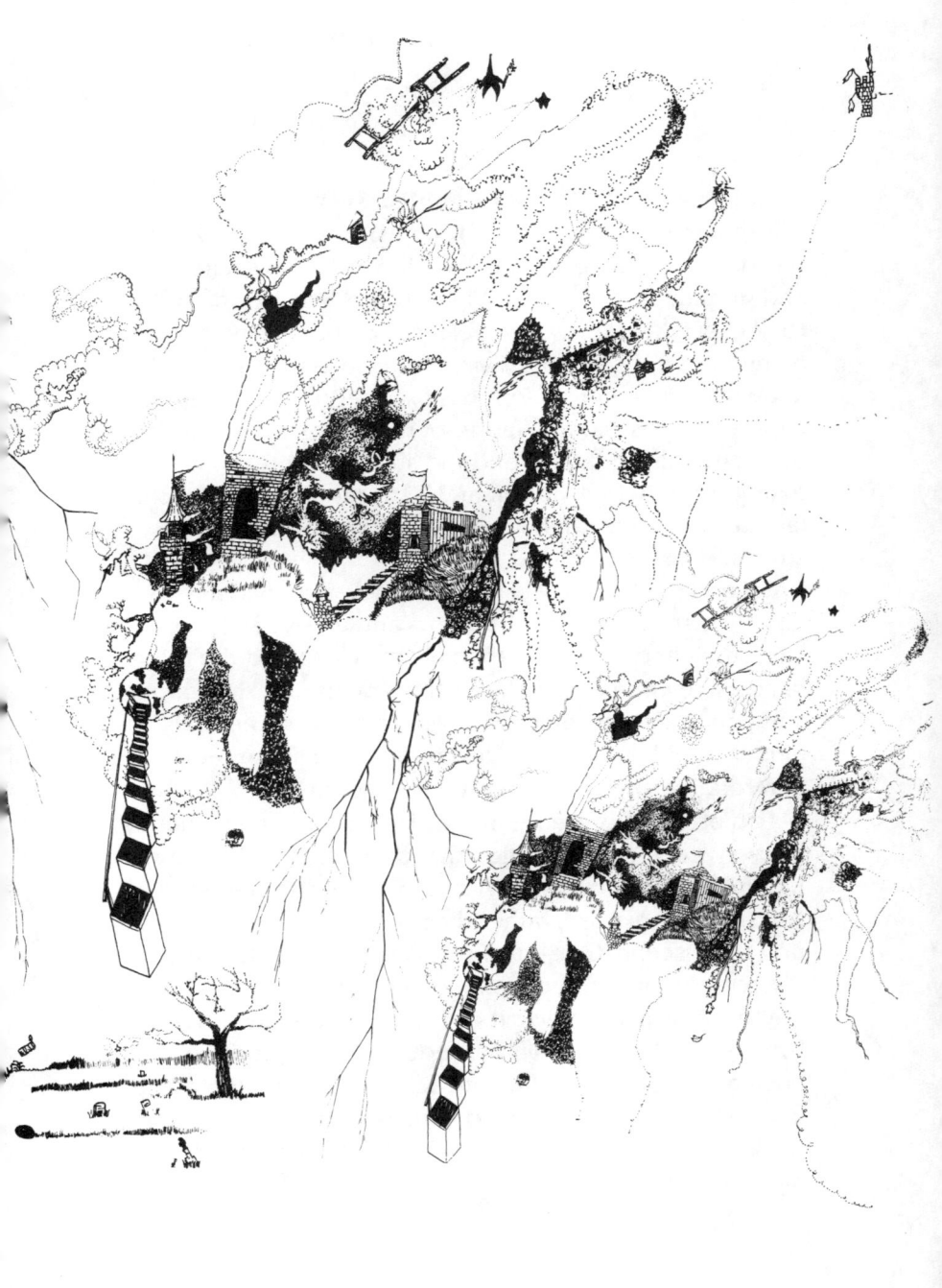

V.
What Am I Doing Here?

Regardless of how perfectly adjusted you are, the first few days are marked by anticipation, nervous excitement and general uncertainty—Where to go, What to do, Who to see, etc. You know the feeling. Fortunately and conveniently there is someone living very close to you who knows the feeling too. Possessing a set of very receptive ears, an extensive knowledge of the campus, considerable problem-solving talents and the ability to detect a fire extinguisher being shot off at 300 yards, this friendly collegiate is often the first link between you and your new surroundings.

Called Resident Advisors[1], these select individuals are generally model college students and always seem to keep their acts together, their rooms clean and their heads screwed on straight. Besides being the kind of person your parents would want you to bring home for dinner, an RA is notorious for making you seem more comfortable and your first days less confusing.

Too often, RA's are treated as Dorm Policemen and not as the wealth of information that they really are. I found it helpful to hunt down an RA as soon as I discovered that such a beast existed, rather than wait for the usual orientation mob-scene. One-on-one, I wasn't embarrassed to ask the barrage of dumb questions that everybody has but that nobody likes to admit not knowing the answers to. Every school has its own procedures for registration, buying books, scheduling, etc. RA's have been there and back—they'll point you, help you, listen to you. For now, think of them as a starting point and count on them as a friend for at least a day.

Making the transition to college life can be a mere jump for some—a real hurdle for others. But everyone goes through some sort of adjustment process—even if it's only learning to live with yellow cinder block walls. If you're one of those lucky few who have it all mapped out and know who you are, where you're going at all times, what you're taking, how much you're going to make when you get out, you probably:
- have read far enough
- are not much fun to hang out with
- are kidding yourself

If you're like the rest of us, you probably:
- will begin to wonder about all sorts of mind-scrambling stuff
- won't always come up with easy answers
- will miss Mom's cooking

As with three million other aspects of college, adjustment is a highly individual affair. There just aren't cut and dry procedures for getting through the deal without a headache, hassle or heartache. I can only tell you that the period exists, that it is characterized by a deluge (or at least a sprinkling) of new thoughts and feelings, and that it ends the same way all the other transition periods in your life end—You grow, you change; you toughen, you broaden.

A good piece of practical (perhaps obvious) advice is not to take on more head battles than you have to. Think generally about where you're headed, but don't get too caught up in finding specific answers. You'll have plenty of time to be concerned about your future. Cramming it all into your first daze is as self-defeating as it is useless. Questions of purpose tend to answer themselves in the long-run and worrying about them to the point of paralysis is a ridiculous approach to your initial development at college.

Choose a course of study that you find somewhat interesting. It doesn't make a lot of sense to spend four years learning about something that you couldn't care less about. If you can't decide between "technical" or "non-technical" studies, go the technical route first. It's much easier to fall from a technical curriculum into a non-technical one, than it is to climb from a non-technical curriculum into a technical one.

Always remember that you're bound to nothing permanently. Ordinarily, majors don't have to be declared officially until your sophomore year. I've seen majors changed as late as senior year. If you're putting the time in and just can't cut it in a particular department, start looking elsewhere.

[1] Resident Assistants, Resident Counselors, Head Residents...something official sounding

Nobody owns his own life. A person whose life doesn't touch another's is a person without a shadow.

—PL

Good humor may be said to be one of the best articles of dress one can wear in society.

—WMT

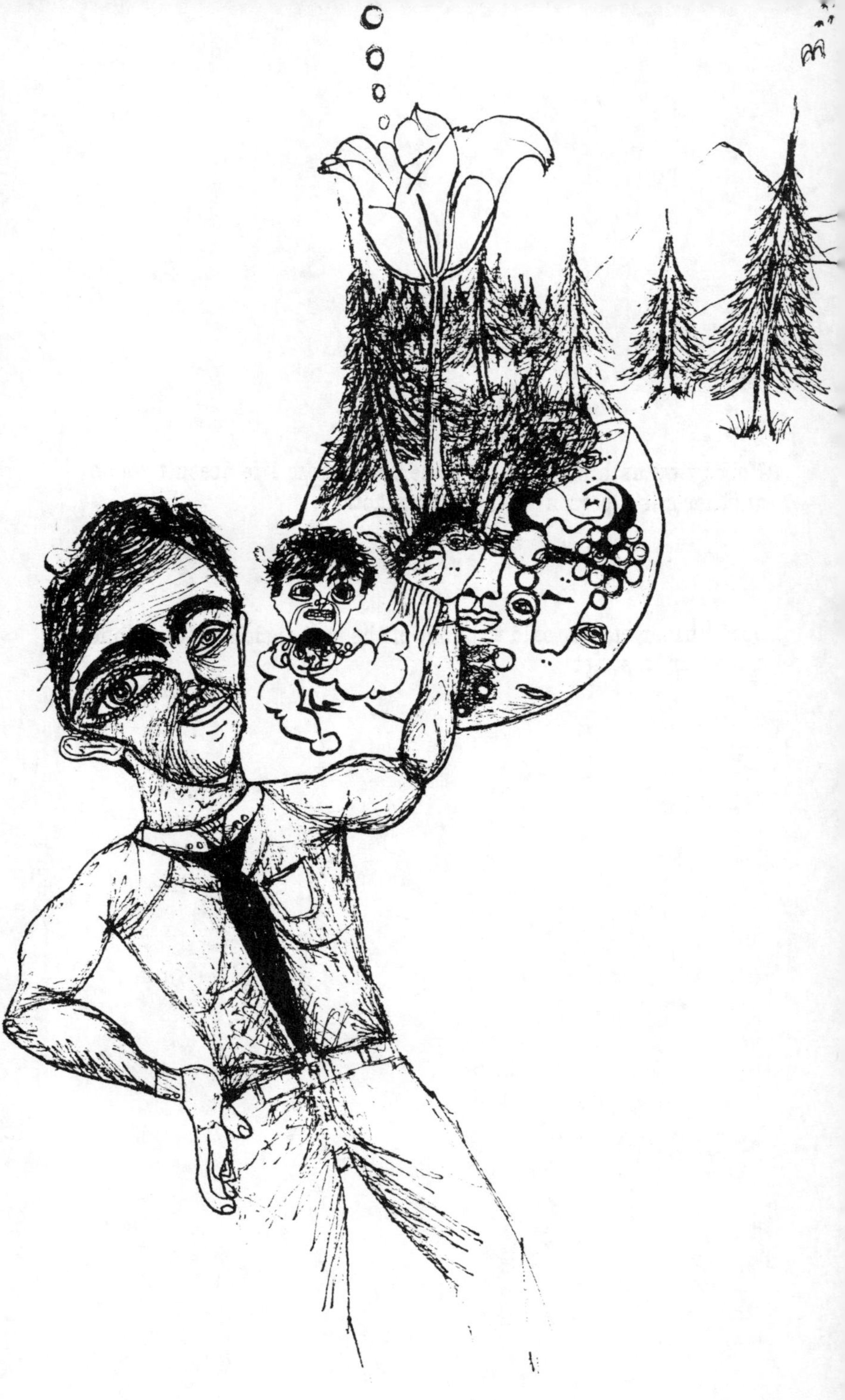

VI.
Friends

You really didn't think that I was going to give you tips on how to act when you meet people. What could I possibly say? Offer them some...Try to remember their...Make sure to mention your...As if you don't have enough common sense to talk bowling with the kid down the hall or pull out your Chipmunk records to break the ice. You know yourself better than I do; I'm not going to insult your intelligence by telling you how to make friends.

Nor am I going to dwell on the obvious point that college—unlike highschool—starts everybody back at square one: No more cliques that were formed back in Kindergarten, no more packs of nerds who won't talk to the muscleheads who won't talk to the freaks who won't talk to the preppies who won't talk to the twinkies, etc. It's a clean slate for now, 'nuff said.

I'm not even going to talk about friends as gateways to sanity in your new home. The food may blow, your mattress may reek, your first class might be before sunrise—you hit on a good bunch of friends at the start and it just doesn't seem to matter as much. But nope, you already know how important those first chumps are.

In fact, I'd have bagged this section altogether if it weren't for the negative effects of first impressions that cause far too many people to put up fronts, misjudge others—or worse yet, go oblivious to each other only to discover friendship at a later date. Wasteful and unnecessary. College is a pool of personalities—a breeding ground for friendship—you can literally go around knocking on doors as soon as you arrive and bring home a bagful of new friends for the asking. And the only thing that stands in the way is that ridiculous shield that some people put up when they're confronted with meeting new faces. You know that shield. The one that keeps you looking pretty cool, but doesn't do a whole lot for your personality. The one that covers up—usually unintentionally—your best qualities and presents others with something that is neither "you" nor what you want "you" to be. A forced front. I don't go by first impressions anymore. I've had too many cocky hard-asses become my best friends.

Quietness is another story. It has its advantages and if speaking when spoken to is your act, you already know them. It's a shame then, that without anything else to go on, people will judge you solely on how you appear to them and then make their own generalization. Staying true to yourself and not giving a crap what others think of you is easier said than done, but I'm convinced that it's worth it in the long haul.

We have a natural tendency to categorize each other according to our own criteria. Not necessarily a problem, but it can be. Versatility is a solution; trying to see parts of yourself in others is another. Never looking or acting exactly the same on consecutive days is still another, perhaps more ridiculous one, but I had fun with it.

Roommates are a special breed of 'first friend' in that you can't just blow them off if they aren't tailor made to your specifications. Unlike with your other friends, you don't always have freedom of selection and escape. Perfectly matched pairs are the exception. Getting to know your new roommate can be your first educational experience or a real nightmare depending on your attitude going into the arrangement. For most of you, this is the first time you'll share a room with a total stranger. Self-sacrifice and compromise—unheard of at home—immediately become part of your college vocabulary. The choicest unmentionables sometimes aren't too far behind.

My case was the absolute extreme. My roommate and I shared no common ground—He was from Stick Country, I was from Concrete County; he was a jock, I pretended to be a musician; he woke up at dawn and made his bed seemingly before he got out of it, I went to sleep at dawn and made my bed only when I decided that I wouldn't be able to find it the next night if I didn't. His side of the room sparkled, whistled AM radio and threatened most self-respecting germs; mine stagnated, blared The Who and threatened most of the atmosphere. But somehow I wouldn't have wanted it any other way. This was my first practical lesson in acceptance of individuality. You know, "Walk a mile in my Docksiders" and all that. It didn't matter that we were perfect opposites, that we didn't hang out together after the first few weeks. We got along; we compromised; we accepted each other's different routines, backgrounds and idiosyncracies. We rarely got on each other's case. And I know I came away better for it— more well-rounded, more broad-minded, more patient with neat freaks, more tolerant of the Village People.

Ours was a ridiculous mismatch—one that we joked about openly. Occasionally, there will be cases that are anything but humorous—where no amount of tolerance is sufficient to keep personal differences from interfering with academics, general happiness, etc. If you and your roommate are just totally incompatible and the situation is unbearable and irrepairable, see the Director of Residence about a change. Eliminate all unnecessary misery from your first year.

I will make you shorter by a head.

—EI

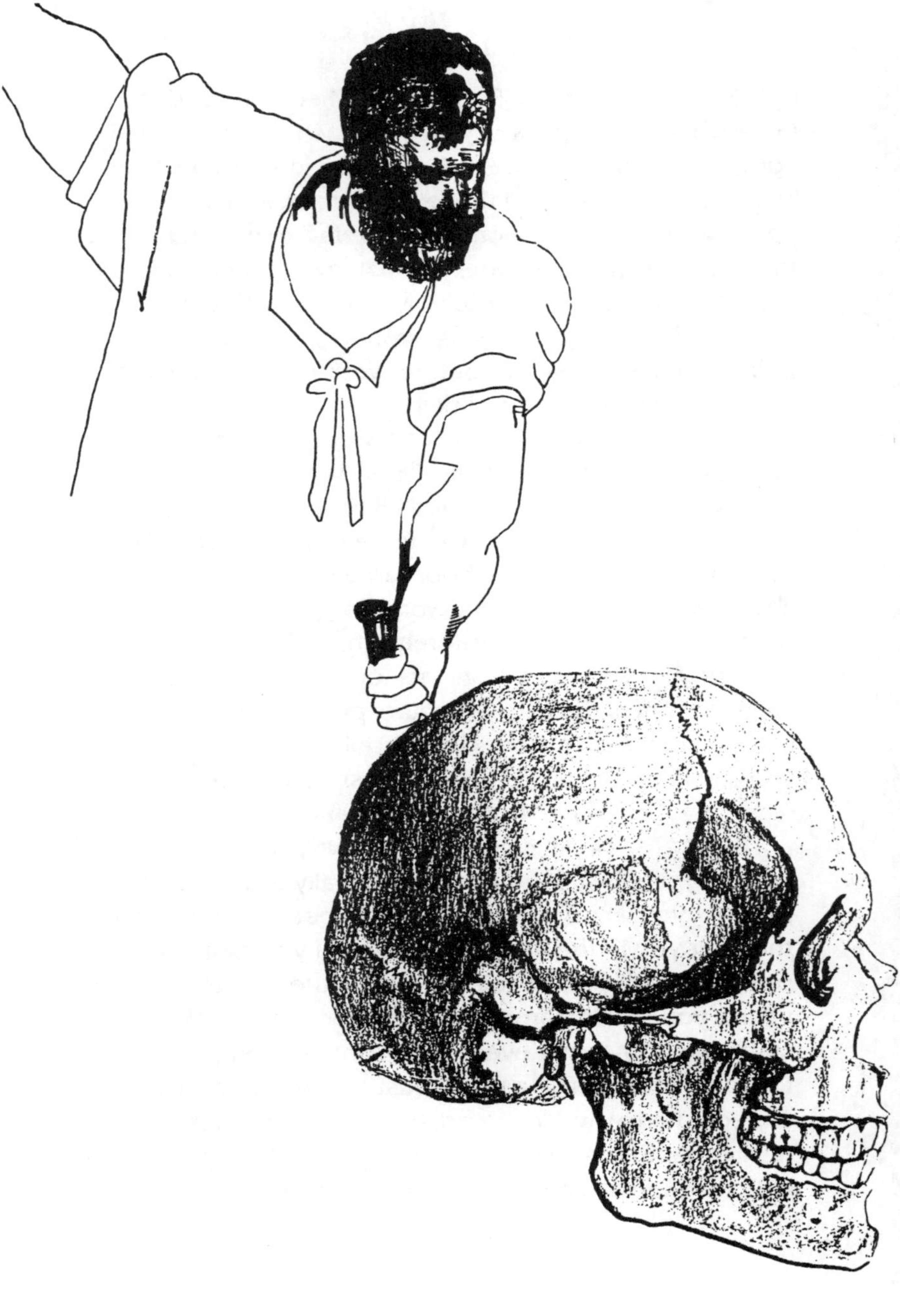

VII.
Work!

    This ain't highschool. Remember when you used to nibble at a few pages a day—when each text chapter comprised several classes of exercises, discussion, little check-up quizzes? Well those days are over. You're on your own now—your workload is going to be intensified; the pressure may overwhelm you. How about a chapter a week? How about two? Multiply that by four or five courses. Being unprepared is expressly forbidden. You're going to have to learn to budget your time and develop efficient, methodical study skills.

    How's that for your typical college academic scenario—courtesy of any Pre-Freshman "Get Acquainted" guide. Makes it sound pretty dismal; as if academic workload were something to get all excited about. I'd worry about holding on to your highschool flame before worrying about being swamped with work. Forget the notion that we're always buried under three tons of books, sweating caffeine, and shriveling from lack of sunlight. The level of college work is right where you expect it to be—it's a natural progression from highschool. You're ready for it; you can keep up with it—the Admissions Office said so when they let you in. That's what they get paid for.

    The degree of difficulty might actually be something of a let down at first. If you went to a really top-notch highschool,[1] you'll find yourself well prepped for anything they throw at you in the early going. Even if you didn't, most professors will spend at least ten minutes reviewing everything you never learned in highschool so that everybody starts out somewhat even. The quantity, though a step up, for sure,[2] is something you adjust to quickly and no doubt expected anyway. Workload soon becomes part of your new expanded routine—expertly getting incorporated in with racquetball, meals, dormitory nanigans, practice and

PASS

evenings of cultural enrichment. Unfortunately, it's sometimes low on the priority list when you have to make time allotment cuts in your daily activities. More clearly, you'll be tempted to bag work first.

This is where the snag occurs most often—the syllabus starts moving towards chapter 10 and you can't see its rear bumper from your stop on chapter 6. Both the beauty and drawback of college is that you're on a self-paced, self-controlled learning system. No one hovers over you with a stop watch. You learn as much as you want to, when you want to, how you....As long as you know it and can prove it two or three times a semester you're golden. But you really do have to know your stuff—tests are, for the most part, challenging, fair, and better indicators than they were in highschool. You can't get away with going in clueless anymore. Cheating is outlawed and penalties often sting a lot worse than mere torn up papers. But somehow cheating isn't even a consideration till later on down the road when you have a feel for the system. But by then you'll feel lousy about violating longstanding academic code and shortchanging your educational experience. Class participation, though a plus and sometimes a nice touch, just doesn't hike your grade the way it used to.

Papers, if part of the course's requirements, can be heavily weighted—it is advisable not to put them off too long. They always take longer than you expect and can be a real eye-opener—particularly if you're not crazy about writing. My first college paper—a masterpiece by my own admission—was slashed and scarred with critical blood by my English 1 prof. The written word is greatly valued and its abuse is not tolerated. Make your point in as few words as possible. What is your point? Think about your audience. Think again. Don't utilize, employ, exert, recur to, make capital of, or use a Thesaurus. Simplicity and clarity are always best. Some people say reading your paper aloud helps detect wordiness—I always feel foolish talking

FAIL

to myself so I have others read my work and then ask for real criticism. Learn to type!

Your first few final exam periods just can't be explained on paper. They're a state of mind. After a while, they'll be just another week of tests. Relax; don't get too excited; they can only ruin your life.

One last note[3]: Don't ever let your workload push you to the point of total despair. It does keep moving; it does pile up sometimes. Keep your sense of humor. You'll find ways to fit everything in; you'll see the sunrise from your desk once in a while; you'll eventually forget 80% of what you're tested on; you'll learn how to learn.

[1] Pennsbury Doughboys
[2] like totally tripendicular
[3] ah

Syllabus

Biology 51
Organism and Environment

T-Th 9:30-10:45
Professor Culesponge

Text: <u>Marketing</u>: <u>Its</u> <u>Origin</u>, <u>Effects</u> <u>and</u> <u>Treatment</u>
by Dr. Dan Key

This course will examine the various strains of plethoric marketing as they affect modern day producers/carriers and the public at large. Lecture will consist of practical application of text material to case studies with an emphasis on diagnostic and operative procedures.

Grading: 1st hour exam, 30%; 2nd hour exam, 30%; final, 40%

Date	Lecture	Chapter
9/4	Introduction	1
6	Aim Toothpaste	
11	Ivory Soap	2
13	Sea Breeze Antiseptic	
18	Bic Razors	3
20	Johnson's Baby Powder	4
25	Toss Toothbrushes	5
27	Influx Cationic Hair Protectant	6
10/2	Cheer Power Pouches	7
4	Tide Multi-Action Laundry Sheets	
9	HOUR EXAM	8
11	Erasermate Pens	9
16	American Heritage Dictionaries	10
18	OFF! Pest Repellent	11
23	Mentor Contraceptives	12
25	Shoe Box Greeting Cards	13
11/1	Magic Mushrooms Air Freshener	14
6	HOUR EXAM	
8	Advent Speakers	15
13	Technics Receivers	16
15	Technics Turntables	
27	Nakamichi Cassette Decks	17
29	Denon Cassettes	18
12/4	Sennheiser Headphones	19
6	Stax Electrostatic Headphones	20
11	OUTERBRIDGE CROSSING Albums	21
13	Jiff Peanut Butter	22

The teacher is like the candle which lights others in consuming itself.

—GR

"Really, now you ask me," said Alice,
very much confused, "I don't think—"

"Then you shouldn't talk, said the Hatter.

—LC

A dragon stranded in shallow water furnishes amusement for the shrimps.

—CP

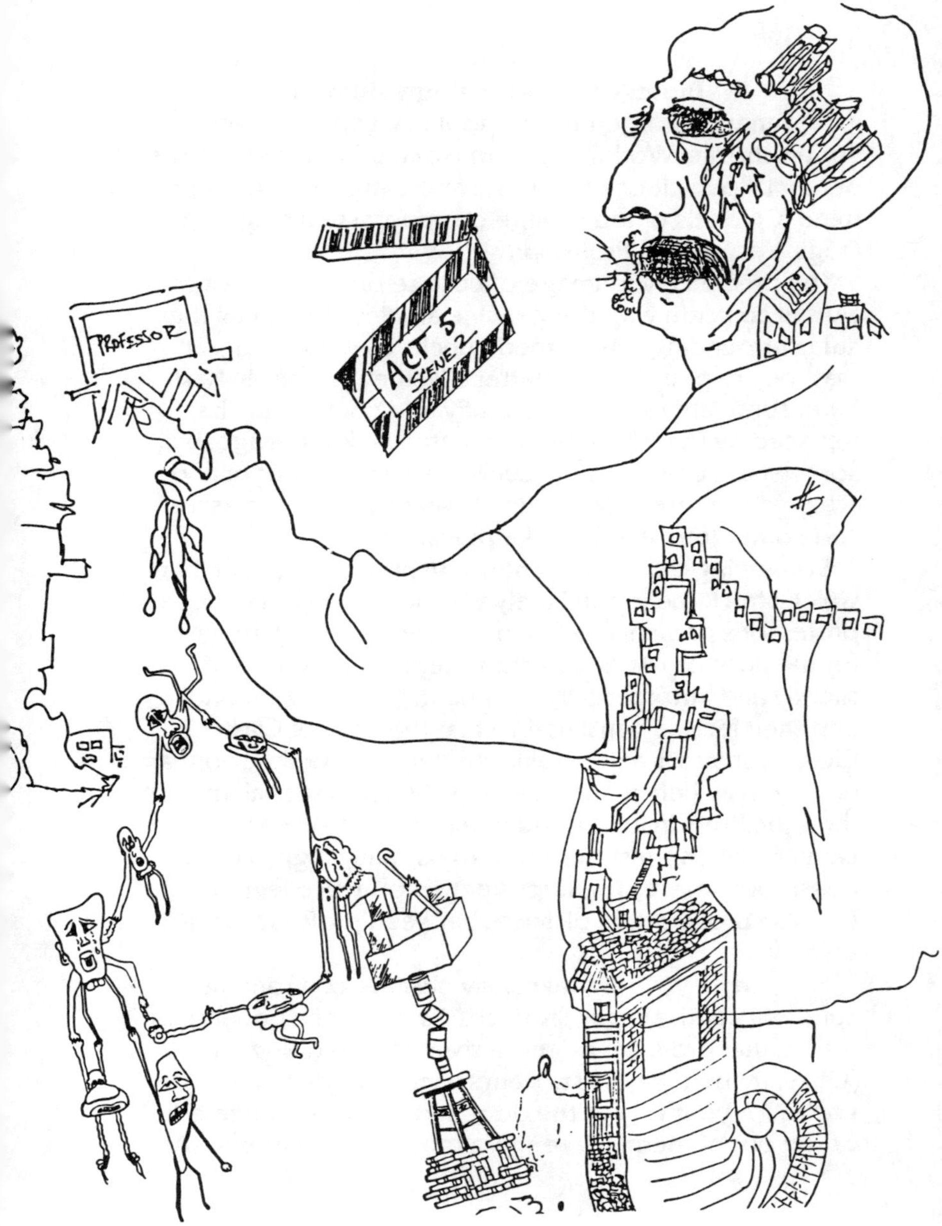
PROFESSOR
ACT 5
SCENE 2

VIII.
Professors: Surprisingly Human

. . . Fanatical, forgetful, Philosophers; sophisticated Superscholars. Worldly wisdom workers dedicated to the perennial pursuit of knowledge and betterment of the mind. Colonels of the college classroom; teaching's Top-Dogs. Yes, sir, Mr. Professor, sir.

The preconceived image of college professors doesn't always coincide with the genuine articles. Amidst all the aura surrounding this learned bunch, it's easy to forget that they're people, too. Better still, they're people **first**. Sure, some are pretentious, stuffy and could easily be replaced by machines. But most are just knowledgeable, somewhat eccentric individuals who enjoy thought and are paid to share it. Many don't wear Clark Kent glasses and some don't even smoke pipes.

Something that you might not think or care about, but which struck me immediately was how quickly a college professor's presence is felt in a classroom. They don't ask for the floor or "Attention Front Center"; they kind of silently and automatically assume it. Not thirty seconds into their lecture you'll realize that the days of Class Clowns, spitballs and breakfast in the back of the room are history. Way before they inspire scholarly, rational, mature thought, Profs inspire good manners. This absence of the carnival atmosphere common to so many high school classrooms makes for surprisingly productive lectures. It can also broaden the distance between professor and student.

For a while you might actually hesitate confronting this curiously captivating individual. Mistake. The sooner you realize that profs are no more than people doing a job (Okay, trained specialists performing a service), the faster you'll kick your foot in the door and really get some education out of them. Make them more than lecturers—Ask for their views; visit them on your own time; Question! Bag the big words; scratch the scholarly hypotheses—Ask 'em about their job. People love to talk about their work. If you're lucky enough to get them rolling, they'll paint a different self-portrait than you might have visualized. They speak regular, usable English; they don't constantly spew out profound, thought-provoking statements; they get a ridiculously lousy paycheck.

The flexible, unpressured lifestyle that is characteristic of college teaching and the ability to work on outside projects, consultations, etc. are the job's main attractions. Not that the whole "joy of teaching" and "spreading of knowledge" idea is necessarily a myth, but it's at best only a slice of the professorial pie. These are knowledgeable people who either can't, couldn't or **didn't want to** cut it in a regular nine to five setting. They opt for the pursuit of their own interests over the regimentation of the rat race.

What this means to you is that you're dealing—not with a superior mind—but merely a very busy one. Smart, but accessible. Be comfortable. Be candid. Underneath what might appear to be an aloof exterior lies somebody that just did their homework.

The prosperity of a country depends, not on the abundance of its revenues, nor on the strengths of its fortifications, nor on the beauty of its buildings, but it consists in the number of its cultivated citizens, in its men of education, enlightenment, and character.

—ML

Facts do not cease to exist because they are ignored.

—AH

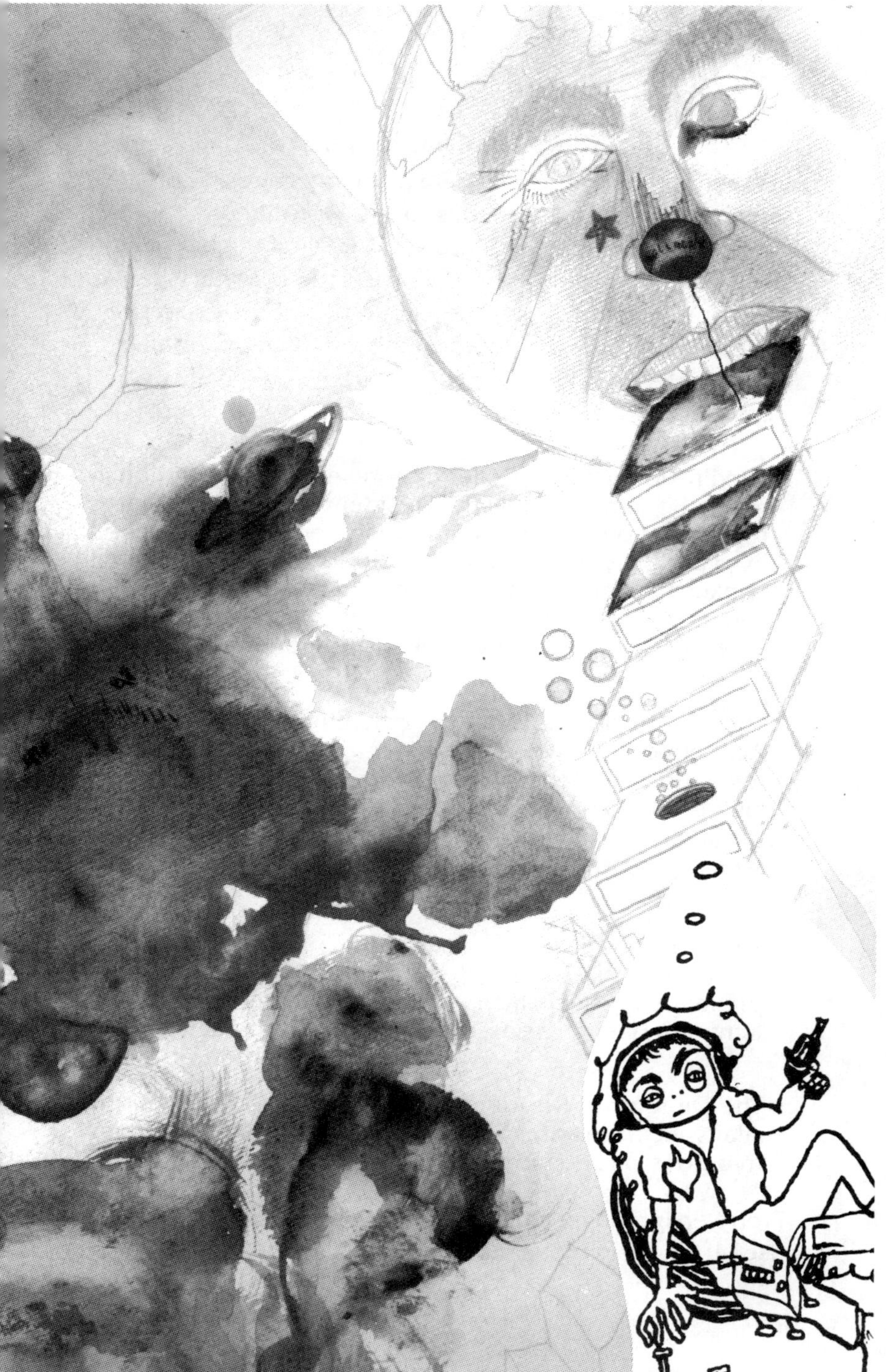

IX.
Who's In Charge Here?

When this chapter was in the planning stages, I considered bringing specific questions over to the administrative offices and interviewing all of the big guns. I was going to run through all of the various administrative positions, giving you brief descriptions of their respective duties, functions, etc. and pawn this off as an informative chapter. Here's a sampling of what you would have been treated to:

> The President of the College represents the institution in much the same way that the President of the United States represents our nation. He or she is a person characterized by diplomacy, tact, aloofness and foresight. He is head spokesman and public relations director, occasionally shows his face at social gatherings, and has a whole arsenal of qualified personnel to do all of the dirty work.

> The Dean of the College concerns his/herself with Academic problems, Academic probation, Academic regulations, Absences, and assorted arelated affairs. It is his/her list that everybody gets all excited about making, but that most people don't feel is worth the sacrifice it entails.

> The Dean of Students deals with Social and Conduct regulations. He or she will cheerfully request your presence in their office when you decide to play food fight, get beer muscles, or do donuts on the Quad.*

> The Director of Residence is responsible for all housing affairs and has a knack for mysteriously knowing everything that goes on seemingly before it does.

Pretty enlightening stuff. And this was supposed to be a useful, entertaining handbook.

FAST

With all due respect for the boys and girls upstairs, I just don't think you're going to give much thought to many of them in your four years. They're nice enough people and all, but they have the loathsome, villainous[1] job of pulling the strings, of making and enforcing the big rules, of looking you squarely in the eye and saying, "I'm sorry, but that's College policy." They don't consciously alienate themselves from the student body—most times they're an exceptionally friendly, helpful group. But chances are you'll be paying them few pleasure visits.

The tendency to associate the administration with law enforcement and authority unavoidably keeps them at arm's length at best. You'll feel a little removed from them; they'll feel a little removed from you and it probably doesn't matter a whole lot. There's a mutual co-existence and as long as you keep your nose relatively clean never the twain shall meet.

What you might want to remember is that—unlike professors—the administration is rarely bendable. These are people with roots firmly entrenched in the educational process. They don't stand in the way of a good time— they just stand in the way of anything or anyone that stands in the way of learning. They give you the benefit of the doubt and treat you like a mature, responsible adult until you prove them otherwise. They're more aware than they let on to be and their punishment has a tendency to hurt.

[1] Two good Thesaurus words
*THESE ARE ALL POTENTIALLY CHILDISH ACTIVITIES AND SHOULD NOT BE ATTEMPTED WITHOUT PROPER SUPERVISION.

HALF FAST

Learning is acquired by reading books, but the much more necessary learning, the knowledge of the world, is only to be acquired by reading people, and studying all the various editions of them.

—LC

What we see depends mainly on what we look for.

—ETP

The man without patience is like a lamp without oil.

—AS

I've got a friend who's a footnote—he tells me what I mean after I say what I don't.

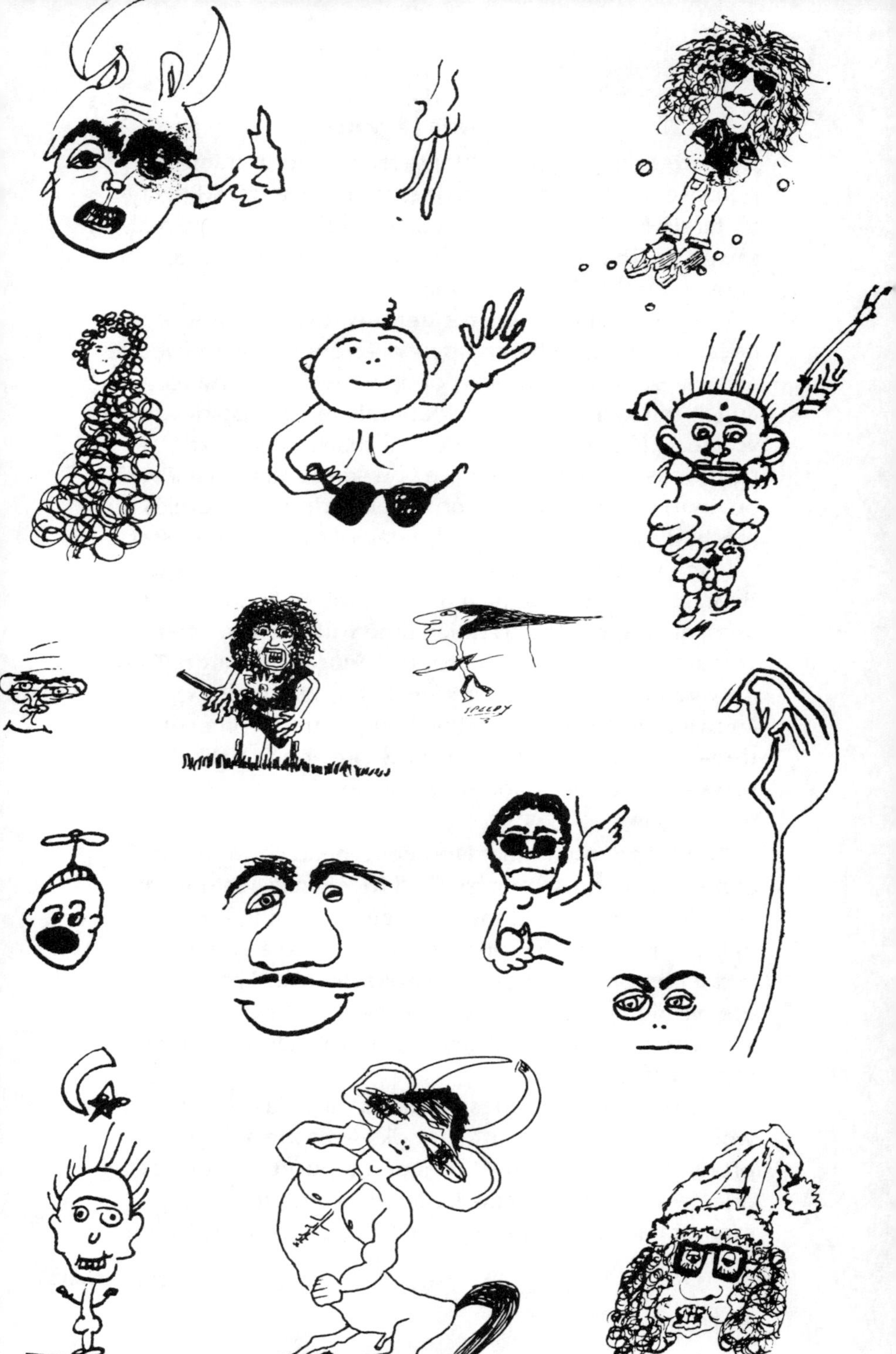
SPEEDY

X.
Friends (Again)

We're talking about the long-term, unforgettable, all-purpose models here. The ones you can laugh with, cry to, fart in front of. The ones you can't lie to, stay mad at, say no to. The ones who know you almost as well as you know yourself. Your Michelob friends.

These full-time playmates get their own chapter because they take on a slightly different role when you're away at school. Regardless of how much importance you attach to studies, you'll undoubtedly reach a point when you realize that there's more to it than a desk and textbooks—when the people you surround yourself with begin to compete with, if not overshadow, academics.[1] I reached this point on the third day of my first semester.

If you've always been a dedicated, conscientious student (and even if you haven't), you might find it hard to rationalize spending so much time with friends. After all, you are (so they say) here for the education. Bingo. **That's** how you rationalize it. For here, in this jungle of knowledge—where food for thought grows on every tree—wisdom also hides in some previously unlikely places. Yes, all of a sudden, even friends become educational.

And I don't mean that Fred Pencilhead down the hall comes over and shares his Fluid Mechanics lecture with you. I'm talking about the real deep, sobering metaphysical thought that only seems to surface when you're in the company of those you hold closest. "Life is an eternal blowjob that doesn't swallow."[2] "You may not see love coming, but you always see it going." "Is money life's report card?"

You won't discuss these topics in any classroom; you won't find them in your textbooks—they're solely the product of intimacy and extended rapport. Besides being priceless, these conversational gems are often more memorable and of more practical value than any formula,

GO AHEAD

graph, table or chair. Show me ten college graduates who know how to take the partial derivative of a fourth order fractional equation and I'll eat that last sentence. Show me another ten who **need** to know same and I'll eat this whole book. Either way, why have only four or five teachers when you can have as many as you like at no extra charge?

Sometimes it's not merely what friends say that is enlightening. Very often the characters themselves—the various attributes, features and idiosyncracies that make them up—force you into inquisition and thought. Being in close company with others for a prolonged period—sharing the same or similar triumphs, setbacks and toilet seats—creates a setting that lends itself to observation and judgement. It might be a bit much to ask you to immediately give up that typically highschool method of judging people on the basis of what you see on the surface. But sometime during your four years you are going to appreciate the advantage of digging deeper. Valuable lessons can be learned from trying to understand other people's stories, why they are the way they are, etc. The qualities you see in those around you and how you perceive them have a funny way of telling you a lot about yourself.

Of course, not all of this wisdom comes without a price. Friendship takes on added responsibility when it is placed in a fixed, close contact, somewhat pressured environment. You'll be exposed to the full range of moods—from the standard "friend" stuff to the crap that used to get taken out on brothers, sisters, parents or the dog. This is something you just learn to accept rather than let bother you—not everyone has the energy and/or desire to always be a live wire at the exact same times as you.

It's no secret that we appreciate things more when we are only able to spend a limited amount of time with them. At college you can spend all the time you want with anything you want—friendship being no exception. It

MAKE MY DAY

becomes easy to lose your perspective—to take for granted those closest to you. I don't claim to know why human nature is such that we think nothing of brushing off our best friends, but immediately put on our best face for acquaintances. Learning to interpret being taken for granted as a kind of compliment isn't always easy. But it really does mean that a person feels close enough to you to bare other sides of their personality.

I'll never fully understand why people prey on each others' weaknesses rather than accept them. Acceptance is the first step to understanding. I guess the smarter and better we become, the harder it is to accept imperfection both in ourselves and others. Realizing that perfection is out of our range gives us the opportunity to constantly grow and improve, but at the same time it enables us to laugh at ourselves. Our inherent beauty is that we have the capacity to recognize our potentials, strive to fulfill them and be ridiculously funny in the process.

Your interaction with others plays a large part in shaping your four years, your life, you. For me, this is what college is all about. For you...Well, for you another choice heads its ugly rear. You can hide in your books night and day—dealing with people only when you have to—and miss out on what I consider to be the heart of a college education. Or you can strike a balance and learn as much as you can from all the various educational sources available to you—books and classes being only a part of the big picture. You can also flip the bird to academics altogether, but then you'll have to write a book or do something equally ambitious to justify four years of screwing around.

[1] slanted statement
[2] Comment inspired by a series of below par test performances

A pile for everything and everything in its pile.

—CK

These go to eleven.

—NT

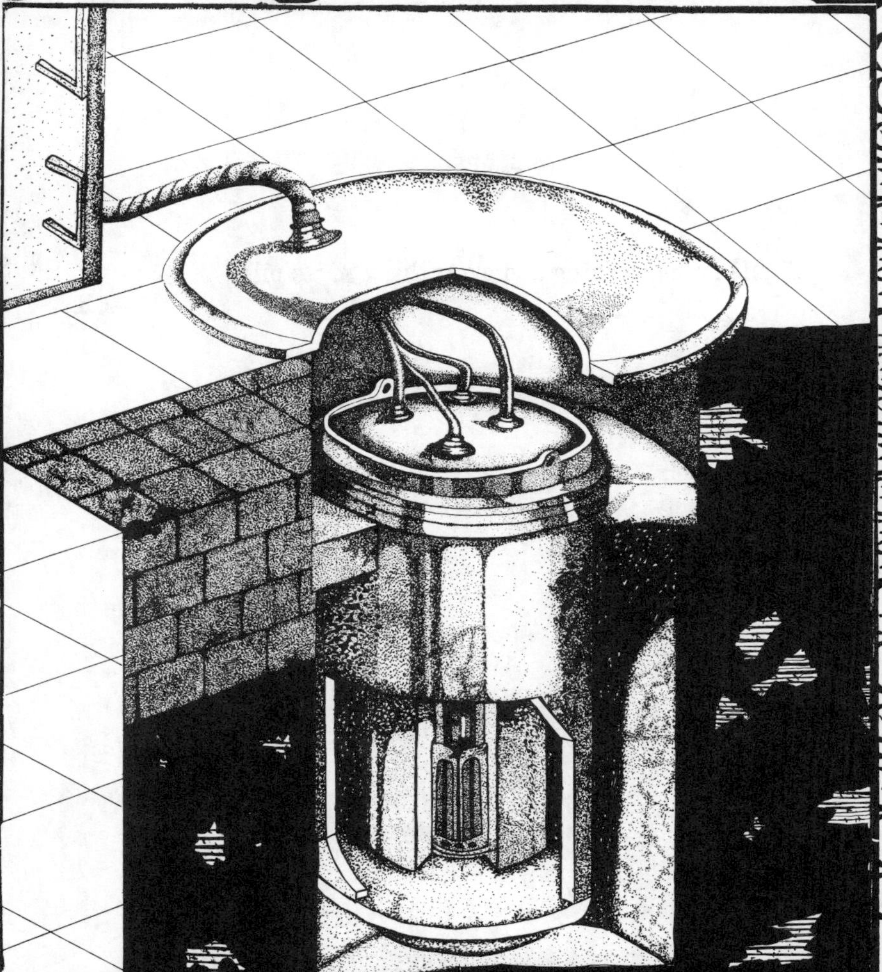

XI.
Bless This Mess

You get a bed, a desk, a chair, some type of wardrobe container, and maybe a couple of shelves. Water color cinder-block walls predominate. It looks a lot like a cell when you arrive. Aesthetics become your responsibility.

Fixing up and adding personal touches to a room is something that just about everybody enjoys. It is during this time that most people really get to know their roommate. What better way to find out about a person than to observe the decor of his/her living space?

Stereos never seem to sound as good at school as they do at home. It probably has a little bit to do with plaster ceilings, cement walls, and Armstrong no-scuff, non-absorbent floor tiles. Rugs, curtains, wall tapestries—they all help dampen hard surfaces and improve mangling room acoustics if you're picky about sound. A graphic equalizer does it all effortlessly if you're picky and rich.

I've seen more stereo speakers rattle off of shelves and come crashing down to their death. If you're into volume, keep speakers on a towel, put a lip on shelves, or afix speakers with double-sided adhesive tape.

Experience the joy of clutter. I've always felt that one of college's greatest pleasures is being able to treat your room like one big walk-in closet. If you're real neat and orderly you'll always know where everything is, but you'll never experience the thrill of unexpectedly finding something you thought was lost forever at the bottom of a pile of junk somewhere.[1]

If you're a total slob, at least set aside general **areas** of your room for related items. At present, I'm not exactly sure where the rest of this manuscript is, but I know it's somewhere in zone three—the area between the end of my desk and my armchair reserved for all unfinished work, unread textbooks, and underwear.

Don't take the bed by the radiator. If you have no choice, stick a glass of water at the base of the radiator to

SOLID

eliminate waking up with the Tahara desert in your mouth. Bunk beds are often available for the asking if you want more space and don't mind running the risk of being luked on some night.

Check out all housing options. Try a year off campus. Living in your own apartment with friends offers an unusual mix of responsibility, independence, and reckless abandon not to be found in any college operated facility. The experience and the different lifestyle far outweighs the occasional feeling of being a little removed from the campus mainstream.

Apartments go fast—it's advisable to start looking for them early second semester. Talk to people who live in them already, check the bulletin boards, check the local obituaries. Read leases carefully. Make sure you're not required to cut and maintain a backyard that is already an overgrown jungle or repanel the downstairs before you leave.

Utilities aren't necessarily included in the rent. We used to let each guy take care of a different bill—One had the electricity bill in his name, one had the phone bill, etc. When a utility bill came in, it was up to the respective individual to figure out who owed what, post the bill, and collect from the other guys. It worked better in practice than it sounds on paper.

Your room is your castle. Friends are at their best when they feel comfortable in the surroundings you provide. I prided myself in having a room that you could spill Bud's in, knock Ray over, and get crumbs on the rug without feeling bad about it.

[1]Sidney Harris

WASTE

FOUR YEARS

A Knucklehead's Guide to College Life

Enter here ye men,
that ye may become better men.

—JP

It's the best house on campus.

Luther told me I could learn something
from you—

I already know how to drink.

—JH

Civilization is overrated.

—S

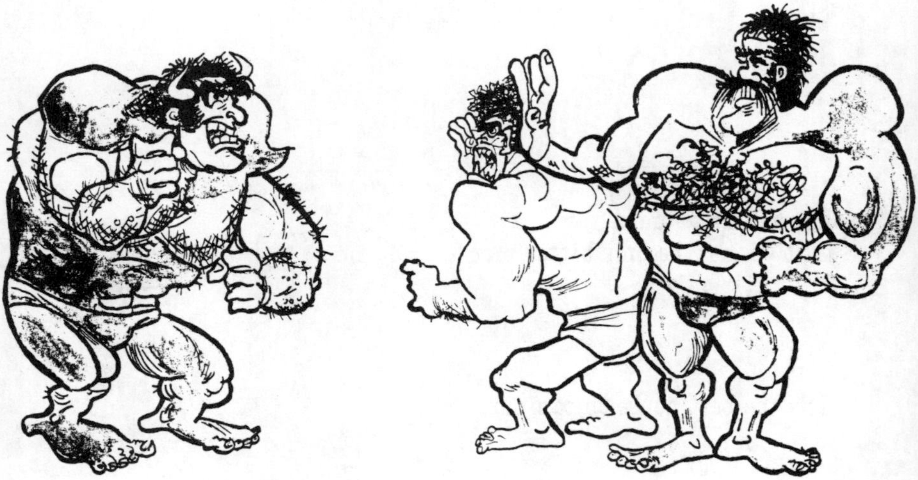

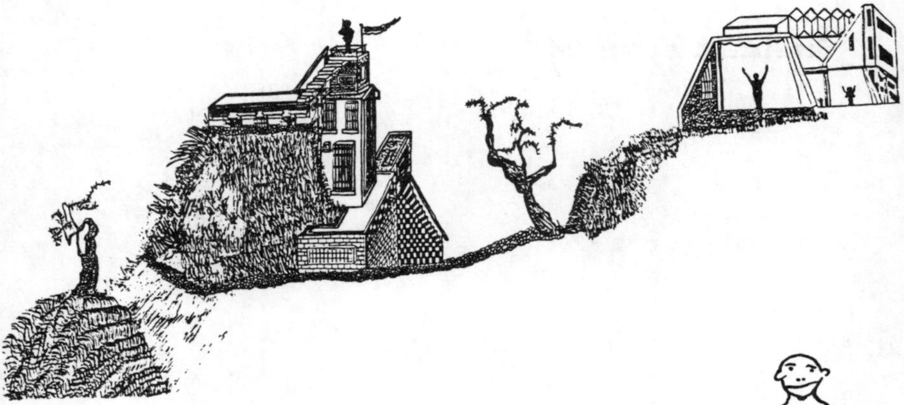

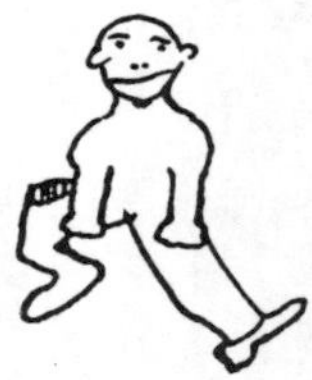

XII.
Fraternities

Dear Mom and Dad,

It's been so long since I've been able to sit down and write a letter—I'm going to knock off the final (and hardest) chapter and say hi in the same stroke. I'm graduating pretty soon and I thought you might like to know what I've been up to, what you've been shelling out bucks for, etc. I've been working pretty hard on something I guess I've always been working on—Learning about people. I've written a very positive account of college based on them. I'm proud of it and I want you to know that I owe most of it to you. (The knuckleheads were constant inspiration).

I used to think that I got along with everybody because of some kind of natural gift. But I've realized that anyone can appreciate people on the level that I do. You just have to be taught that there's an advantage to it. It seemed so obvious to me for so long that I forgot where I learned it from. You are two of my favorite teachers and if enjoying everybody was part of your lesson, I've learned.

I wish I could explain all of the things connected to this fraternity, but there's so much to it and you have to actually live it to appreciate it. It was easily the most fantastic part of my life and will probably be the most memorable. Besides being a country club and a foul den of heathens, it's an educational utopia. It's hard to go through one totally unaffected. You can't help but learn and sometimes it's so painless you don't even realize it. Even when the learning stings a little, it's still useful knowledge. I tried to take part in as much as I could and I learned from everyone. Sometimes it's hard to be friends with everybody, but I worked at it and I'm glad I did. I'm trying to pass on some of your infinite wisdom and I hope you're not sore that I plagiarized a lot.

I'm all your fault—this place just honed me into something I now know what to do with. It could be just about anything and it might well be. I've always known I was pretty smart, but I'm starting to think I'm very smart. Whether I've got life by the balls remains to be seen...

You cranked out a talented, confident, versatile knucklehead who'll always be content not knowing what's next. If I don't always speak it, it's because I assume it's understood.

Love,

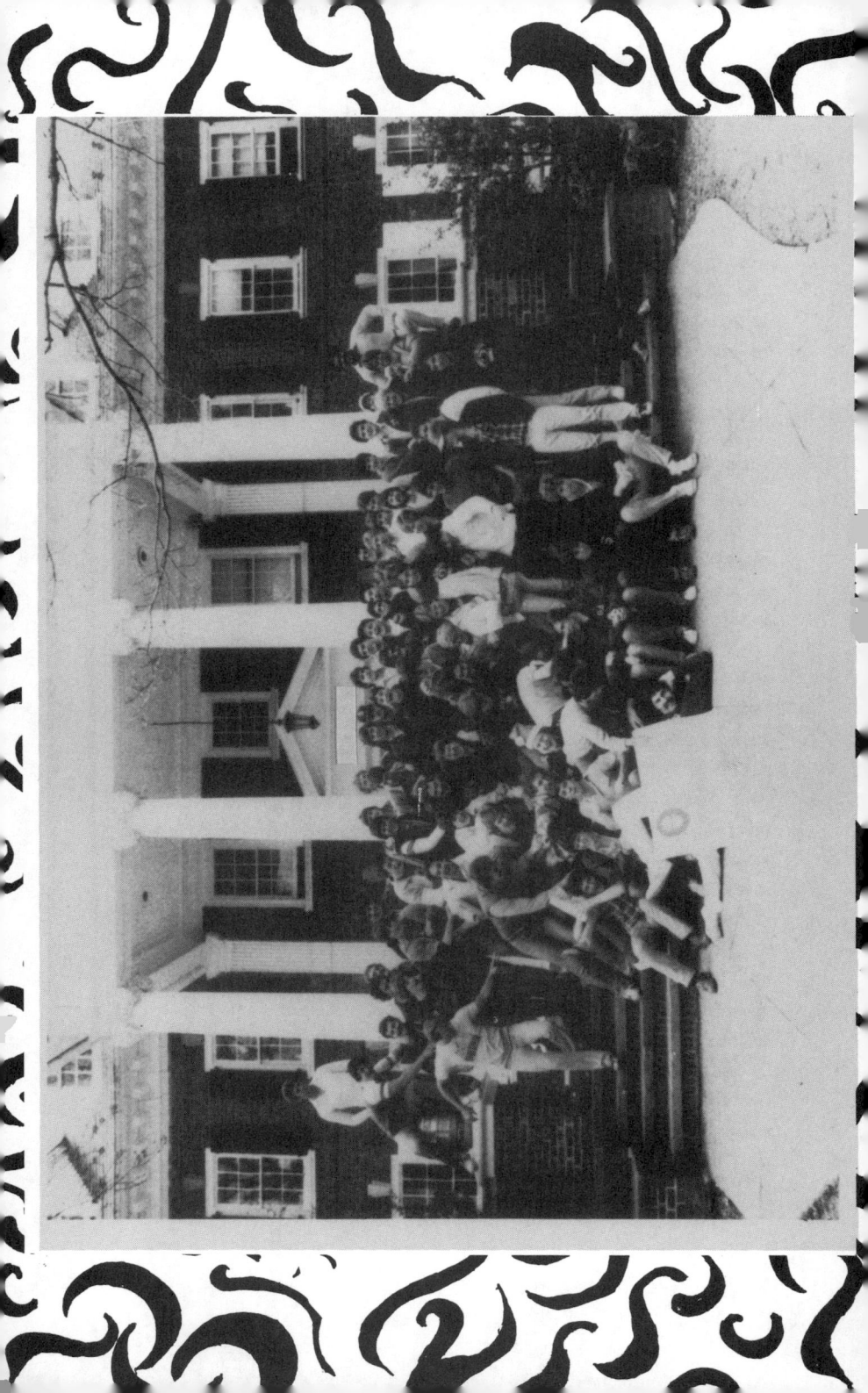

Tradition shouldn't be the enemy of innovation.

—ARP

You don't have to be born with balls to have them.

—GDI

Great spirits have always encountered violent opposition from mediocre minds.

—AE

Surely, comrades, you do not want Jones back?

—S

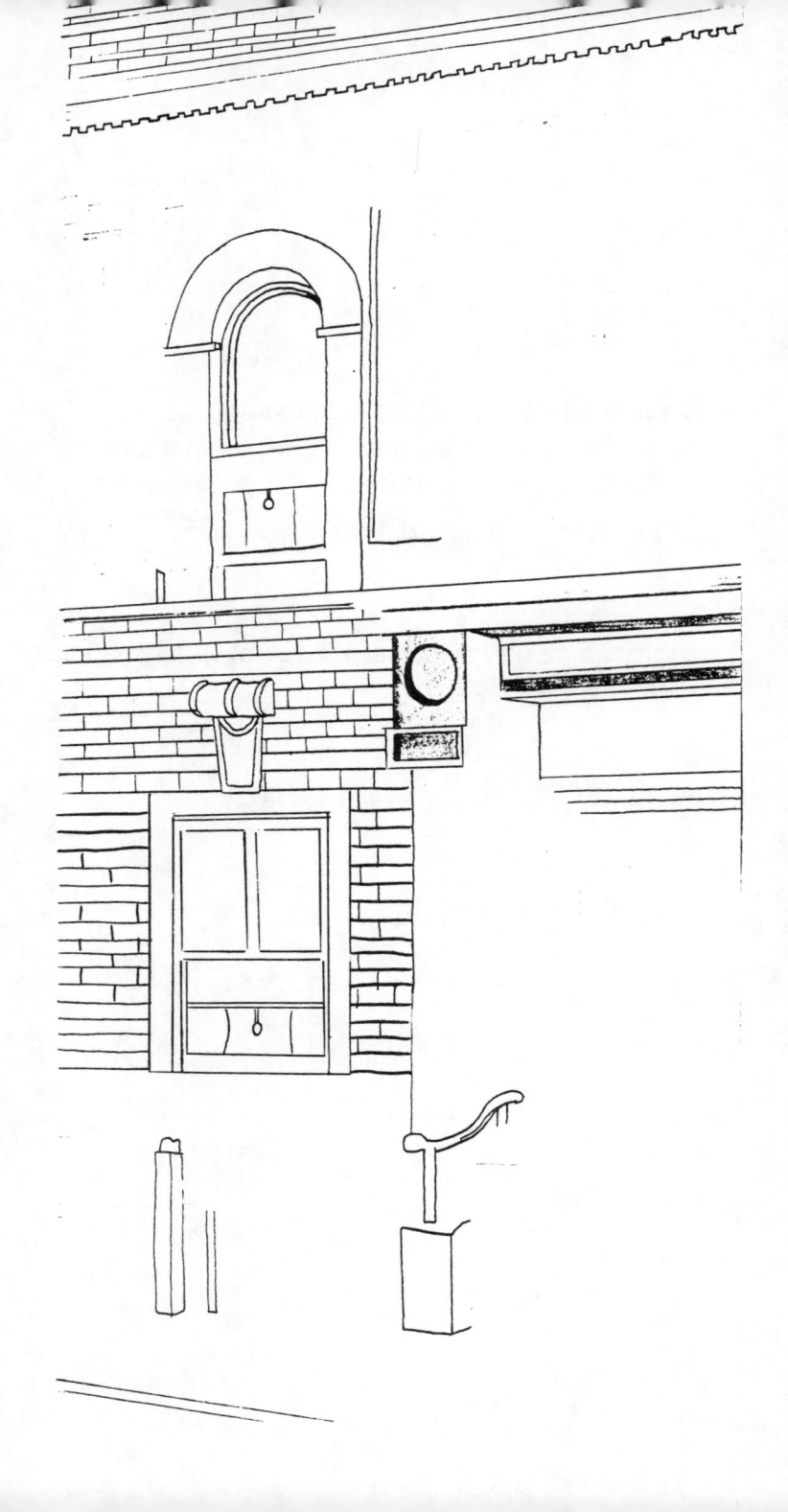

XIII.
Sororities

Tough chapter. I can't write about everything objectively. This would be like trying to write about the Ladies room in third grade. You know that things probably are basically similar and a lot of the same stuff goes on, but still something's different. Why can't difference be great?

It's harder now—you gotta plan more, you gotta prepare more.

—BC

This time, you're going to lose.

—RM

All's fair that ends well.

—BB

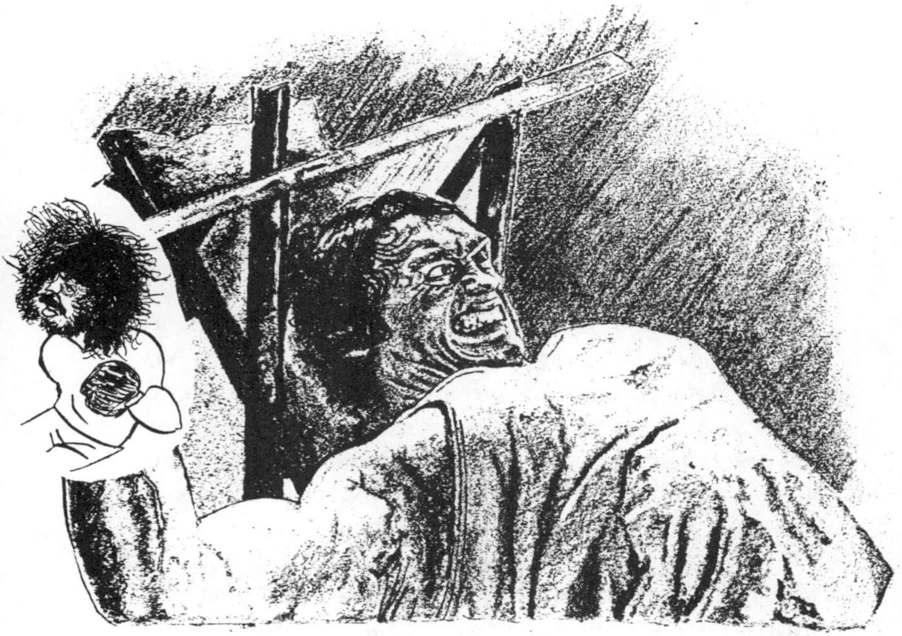

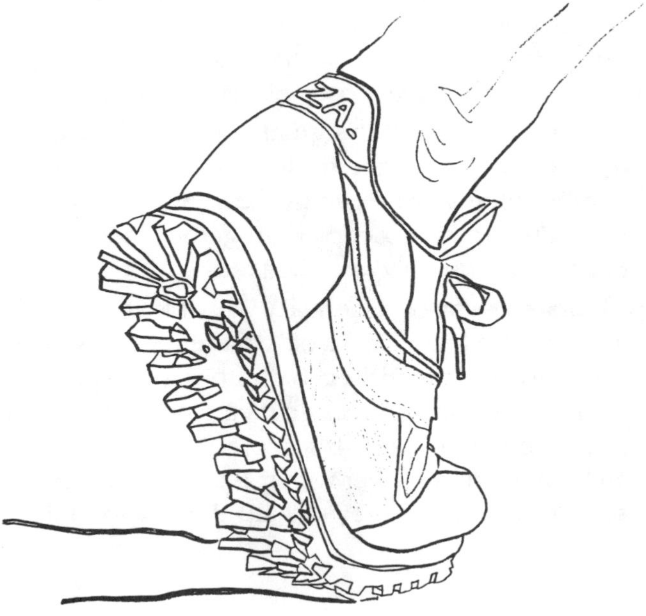
ZA.

XIV.
Sports

Competing for the top spot on the list of "Greatest Fringe Benefits of College" is Sport-Ease.

Sport-Ease n.—the ability at virtually any hour to engage in or round up willing competitors for various types of athletic pursuits

Racquet ball at 9:30, hoops after lunch, street hockey until dinner, darts at Phi Psi, cup-pong till all hours. No longer are pick-up games, matches and workouts confined to the four to six after-school slot. Don't ever let anyone tell you that the academic life and the sporting life are mutually exclusive. College is a gamesman's heaven—a playground for knuckleheads.

Potentially....lousy sleeping habits, too much talking to Ray, ten page papers, Jack, slime crew detail, junk food—they all contribute to physical deterioration and sometimes make voiding[1] an easy endurance sport. Often the acceleration of the mind leads to the decceleration of the body. Guys go soft; girls can't get into their Calvin's anymore. It happens.

So that you're not out of shape by Thanksgiving, I'm recommending liberal doses of the following:

Hoops—Still one of the greatest sports for working last night out of your system. I'll always be amazed at the number of guys who can go from incoherency at night to tearing up full court pick-up games the next day. Two bounce for the truly anesthetized.

Ultimate Frisbee—Essentially "downless" football with a frisbee. One team "kicks off" to the receiving team who can't run with the frisbee, but rather moves down the field with a series of consecutive passes. A completed pass into the endzone is a score. An incomplete pass is an immediate turnover with the other team taking possession as soon as they pick up the dropped disk.

THE GREAT

There's a 'stalling' rule on offense that's flexible, rarely needed and not worth explaining. Field size is arbitrarily related to number of participants and desire to suck wind. Everybody's a star—ex-monsterbacks, line up comics, time budgeters, point sponges, cherry pickers and shroomies alike.

Pool—The quintessential college game—seems like everybody comes back a better player. You can't say "Hercules never won a pool match" seriously anymore, but it's still a good tip. Making up knucklehead games when all we had were bad tips was temporarily entertaining.

Street Hockey—Use the tennis courts when the nets are down. Bring a crummy pair of gloves from home.

Racquet Ball—The second favorite cold weather indoor sport for two.

Golf—If you shoot anything under three digits and love to play, try out for the golf team. Even if you're a hacker, you stand a shot at free playing time. "Campus Nine"[2] when you can't make it to the course. Hallway rug putting available at some schools.

Ping-Pong—No longer a sissy game. If you play fairly regularly, the game builds up a unique intensity and your hand-eye coordination will improve in other areas—Darts, racquet ball, three on three, frisbee and opening doors to name a few.

Bowling—With friends and some pitchers for an occasional joke if nothing else. Low scorer for designated frames buys the next round.

Darts—The aerial equivilent to pool: moderate energy expenditure stressing hand-eye coordination and offering instant, fleeting prestige to the proficient. "Baseball" is to darts what "Eightball" is to pool. An English game called "Cricket" requires more talent and strategy but is virtually impossible to explain clearly on paper. Ask a dart hound—there's one in every crowd.

THE LATE

Frisbee Golf—Start anywhere; stop anywhere—"Holes" are oak trees, lamp posts, statues and mailboxes. Par for each hole is arbitrary and arguable.

Of course, the obvious stuff needs no description or explanation. Running with the rap killers, lifting, tennis matches with the poaching pirahnas, softball games with the diamond dogs, mud football marathons with all the animals and other assorted athletic endeavors are always worth the effort it takes to get them in gear. Sports make us kids forever.

[1]voiding—act of filling central nervous system with less than the adult minimum daily requirement. Not necessarily linked to amount of television time logged, but a correlation does exist. Produces mental state characterized by listlessness and decreased sensory awareness.

see also: inactivity, counterproductivity, general hospital, voring, oarheads, homebox

[2]Frisbee Golf Rules

***Joe, Ya Coulda Made Us Proud**—Joe Pepitone
The Year The Mets Lost Last Place—Dick Schaap
                                    —Paul Zimmerman
Life In The Pit—Deacon Jones
Winners And Losers—Sidney Harris
In Search Of Excellence—Tom Peters
Innovation and Entrepreneurship—Peter Drucker
Hit #29—Joey

THE WORLD ALMANAC

Bridge On The River Kwai	Taps	The Final Option
The Longest Yard	Walking Tall	Papillion
Where Eagles Dare	Ben Hur	Duel
Patton	Deliverance	Rolling Thunder
Heaven Can Wait	Thief	Endless Summer

We got you the education I never had, so use it to appreciate the leisure that goes with it.

—L

Life's a beach.

—BS

The charm of fishing is that it is the pursuit of what is elusive but attainable, a perpetual series of occasions for hope.

—JB

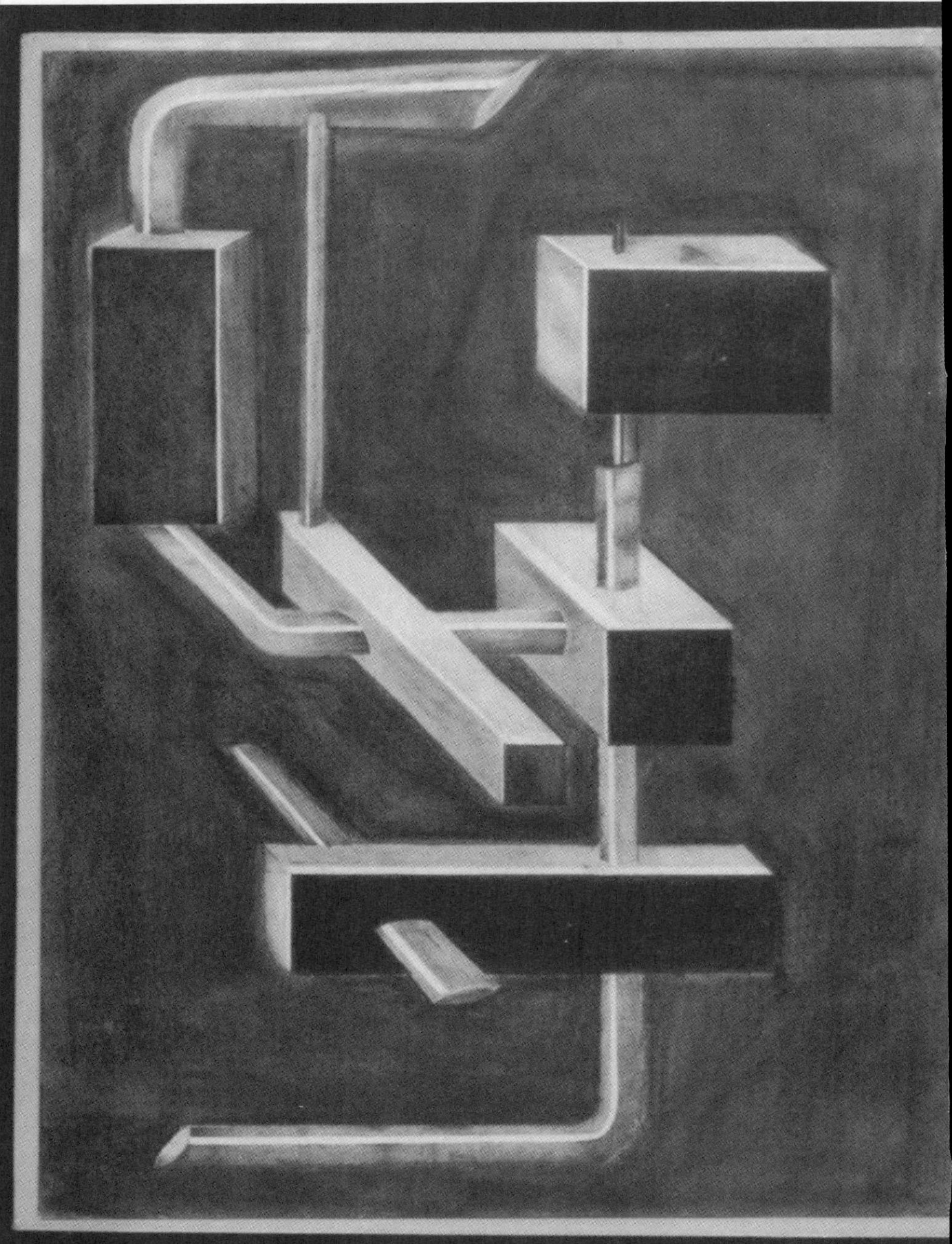

XV.
Recreation

Even though I've dealt with one form of recreation in chapter 14, here I'm making a very clear distinction between sports and recreation. Ideally, some type of purely athletic activity should always be part of your daily routine. Sound body—sound mind, as they say on the Wheaties box. I can't campaign enough for sports, they're still the greatest, most practical mind-freeing excursion available to modern man. But occasionally you should do something special—a little out of the ordinary—something that resembles a miniature vacation.

It's a real marvel that the mind has virtually no bounds—that with regular use its capabilities just continue to mushroom.[1] The effects of constant mental gymnastics are immediately apparent, obviously advantageous, and pretty remarkable. And tedious at times.

It's easy to appreciate how mentally fried you can become after the occasional hectic week of tests on top of lengthy reading assignments on top of a paper or two. But that's just battle fatigue—short term stuff—it goes away with time and rest. It's perhaps harder to foresee the long term effects of intense and prolonged exposure to a college education. You become so trained to think analytically, to question constantly, that you end up developing a mind that's almost always spinning. That's good. Occasionally, you just want to turn it off and can't find the switch. You just can't kill the mental process the way you flip out a light. You start to look at a stapler 500 different ways and contemplate the relative merits of video games. That's tedious.

This is when you appreciate the benefits of recreation—of getting the hell out of Dodge. Take a bike ride, hit the slopes, go on a picnic, go mudsliding, go fishing, go canoeing, Go! Discover the great outdoors! T.R. once said,

ZOOM

"The farther one gets into the wilderness, the greater is the attraction of its lonely freedom." Hiking and camping out on weekends are things we did far too seldomly and always seemed to enjoy the most. They free the mind and beckon a return to simplicity. The outdoors has a subtle, yet curiously effective way of reminding you that the purpose of life is to enjoy it.

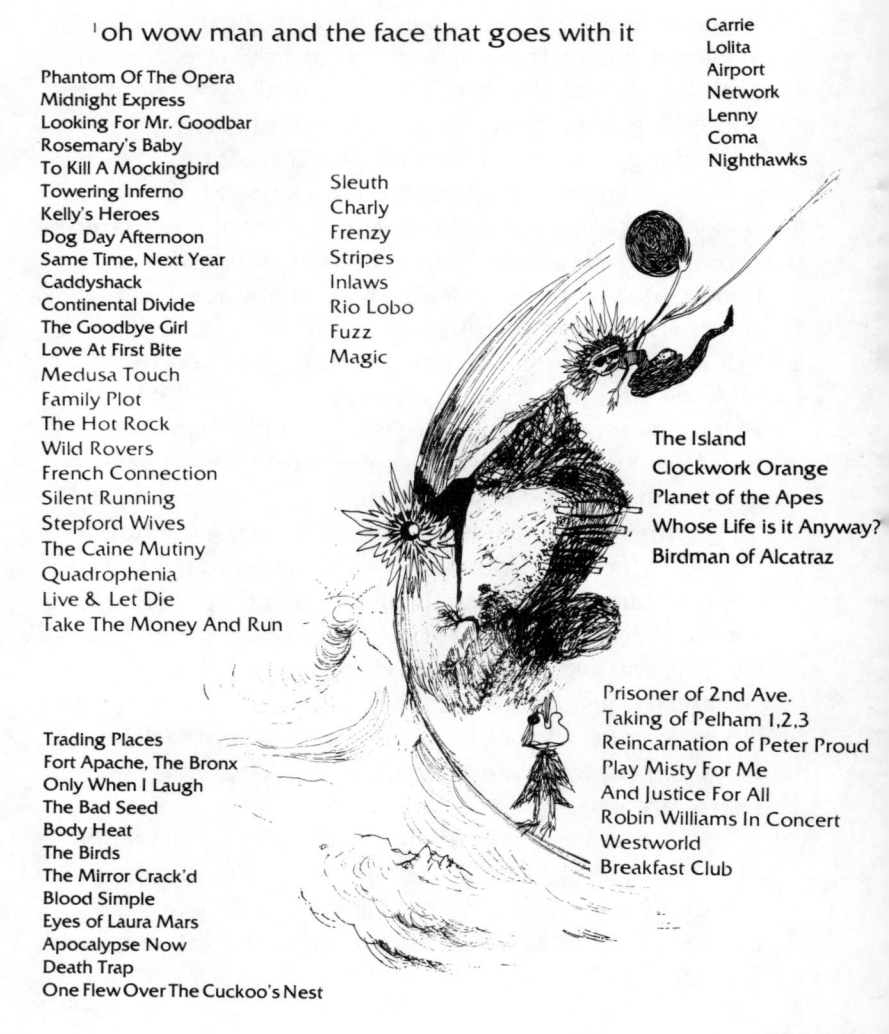

[1] oh wow man and the face that goes with it

Carrie
Lolita
Airport
Network
Lenny
Coma
Nighthawks

Phantom Of The Opera
Midnight Express
Looking For Mr. Goodbar
Rosemary's Baby
To Kill A Mockingbird
Towering Inferno
Kelly's Heroes
Dog Day Afternoon
Same Time, Next Year
Caddyshack
Continental Divide
The Goodbye Girl
Love At First Bite
Medusa Touch
Family Plot
The Hot Rock
Wild Rovers
French Connection
Silent Running
Stepford Wives
The Caine Mutiny
Quadrophenia
Live & Let Die
Take The Money And Run

Sleuth
Charly
Frenzy
Stripes
Inlaws
Rio Lobo
Fuzz
Magic

The Island
Clockwork Orange
Planet of the Apes
Whose Life is it Anyway?
Birdman of Alcatraz

Trading Places
Fort Apache, The Bronx
Only When I Laugh
The Bad Seed
Body Heat
The Birds
The Mirror Crack'd
Blood Simple
Eyes of Laura Mars
Apocalypse Now
Death Trap
One Flew Over The Cuckoo's Nest

Prisoner of 2nd Ave.
Taking of Pelham 1,2,3
Reincarnation of Peter Proud
Play Misty For Me
And Justice For All
Robin Williams In Concert
Westworld
Breakfast Club

BOOM

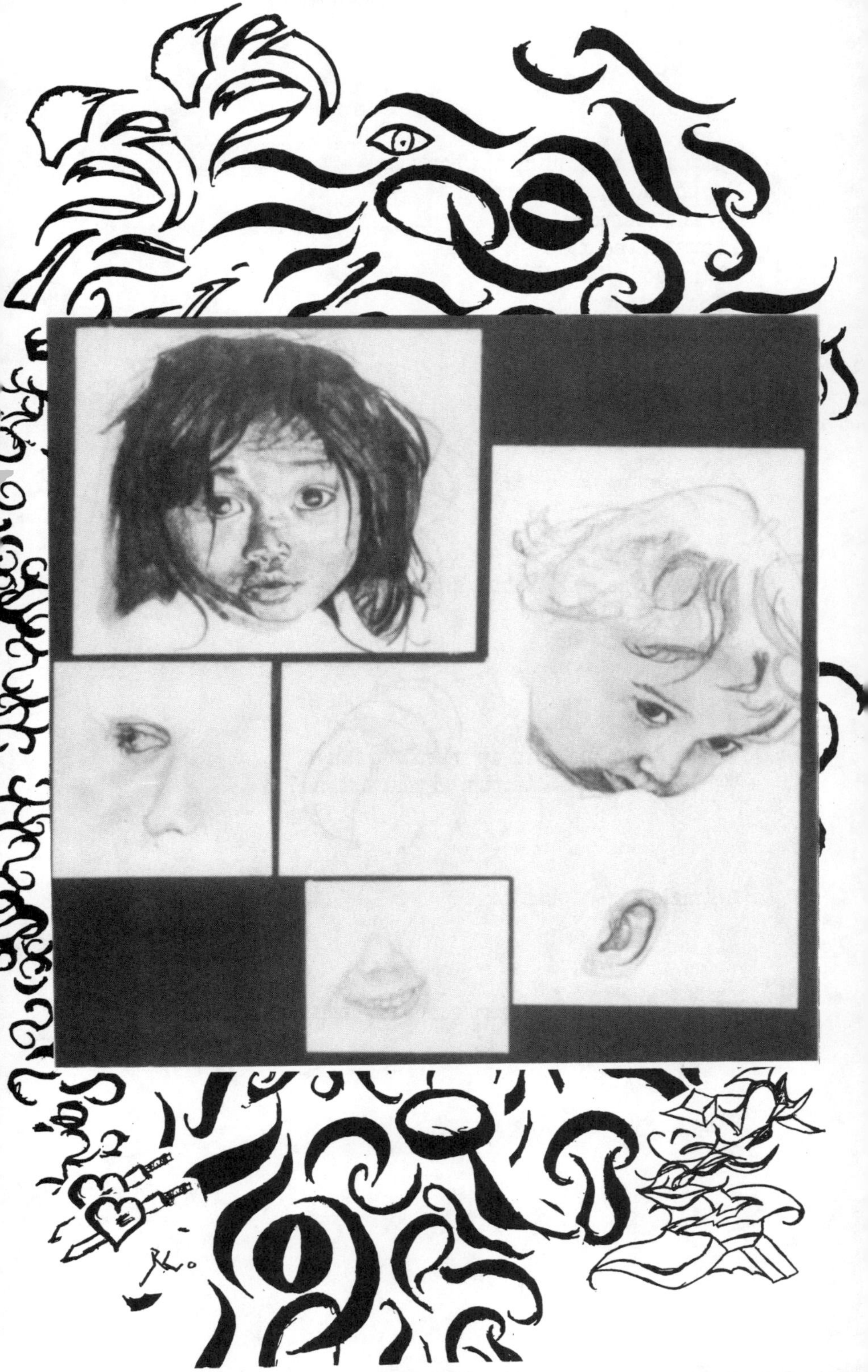

I saw a man pursuing the horizon
Round and round they sped.
I was disturbed at this;
I accosted the man.
"It is futile," I said
"You can never...
"You lie," he cried
And ran on.

—AU

I should've kept the rib.

—A

To find a queen without a king
they say she plays guitar
and cries and sings.

—RP

Who's gonna pick you up when you fall
Who's gonna pay attention to your dreams?

—BO

Animals have rights, too.

—HS

Without any money there goes our romance.

—D

Why are you running away?

—P

I think that you have a lot to learn about merchandising.

—E

Will my heart be broken when the night
meets the morning sun?

—CK

You needn't feel too badly, Wilbur. Not many
creatures can spin webs.
Even men aren't as good at it as spiders,
although they think they're pretty good,
and they'll try anything.

—C

Only women bleed.

—AC

Don't it always seem to go
that you don't know what you've got
till it's gone.

—JM

So this is love?

—DLR

You were under the impression
that as you were walking forward
you'd end up further onward
but things ain't quite that simple.

—PT

XVI.
Sex...

Sex, drugs and rock & roll. A convenient way to give three chapters names and nothing more. I don't subscribe to the counter-culture religion that is normally associated with this powerful, anti-establishment statement of defiance. I don't think anyone says it with a straight face anymore.

This is a chapter about relationships. Boysland and Girlsland. Sexual freedom. Values. Bias. Acceptance. Respect. I wish I had a lot of profound things to say about all of this stuff, but the more I think about them, the more subjective and abstract they all become. I think that's why I'm having so much trouble writing this chapter. The harder you try to answer every unanswered question, the more you just want to go out front and play wiffleball.

I worry that drugs have forced us
to be more creative than we really are.

—LT

I think this drug business will destroy
us in the years to come.

—VC

I told you that shit'd make you ignorant.

—GP

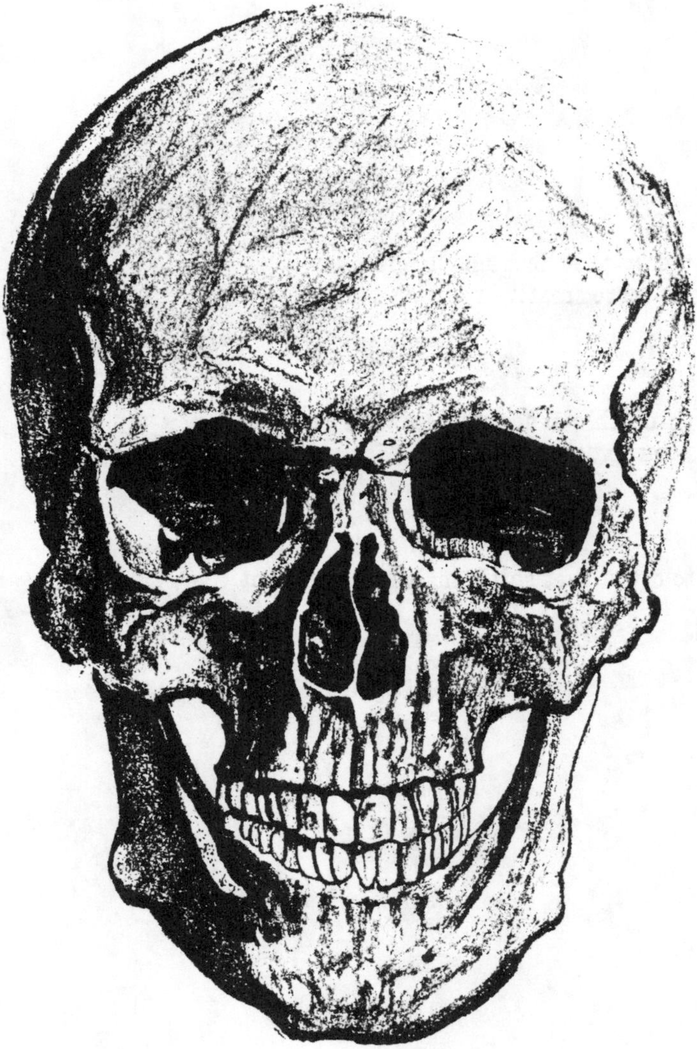

XVII.
Drugs

There is a path not yet taken
  will lead you down it
Across the unfirm terrain,
Along its winding course,
In search of the new, the unique, the undone.

Together we press on—
For at the end of our trek lies
Neither fame nor glory
But something far greater.

For no man has yet ventured onto this ground,
None have yet dared to step in these tracks—
And we have.
We care not where the path leads,
Only that it is, as yet, untravelled—
And we are the first.

The footing's unsure,
We're stuck at times;
Yet we push on.
For our journey is near complete;
And we smell success.

Oh the self-satisfaction, the peace of mind,
To proudly stand
And look back at our tracks
In the wet cement
Of the freshly laid sidewalk
Leading to the shitpile
At the manure factory.

If a man does not follow his companions
perhaps it is because he hears
a different drummer
Let him step to the music
he hears
however measured or far away.

—HDT

Imitation is the sincerest form of larceny.

Shut up and play yer guitar.

—FZ

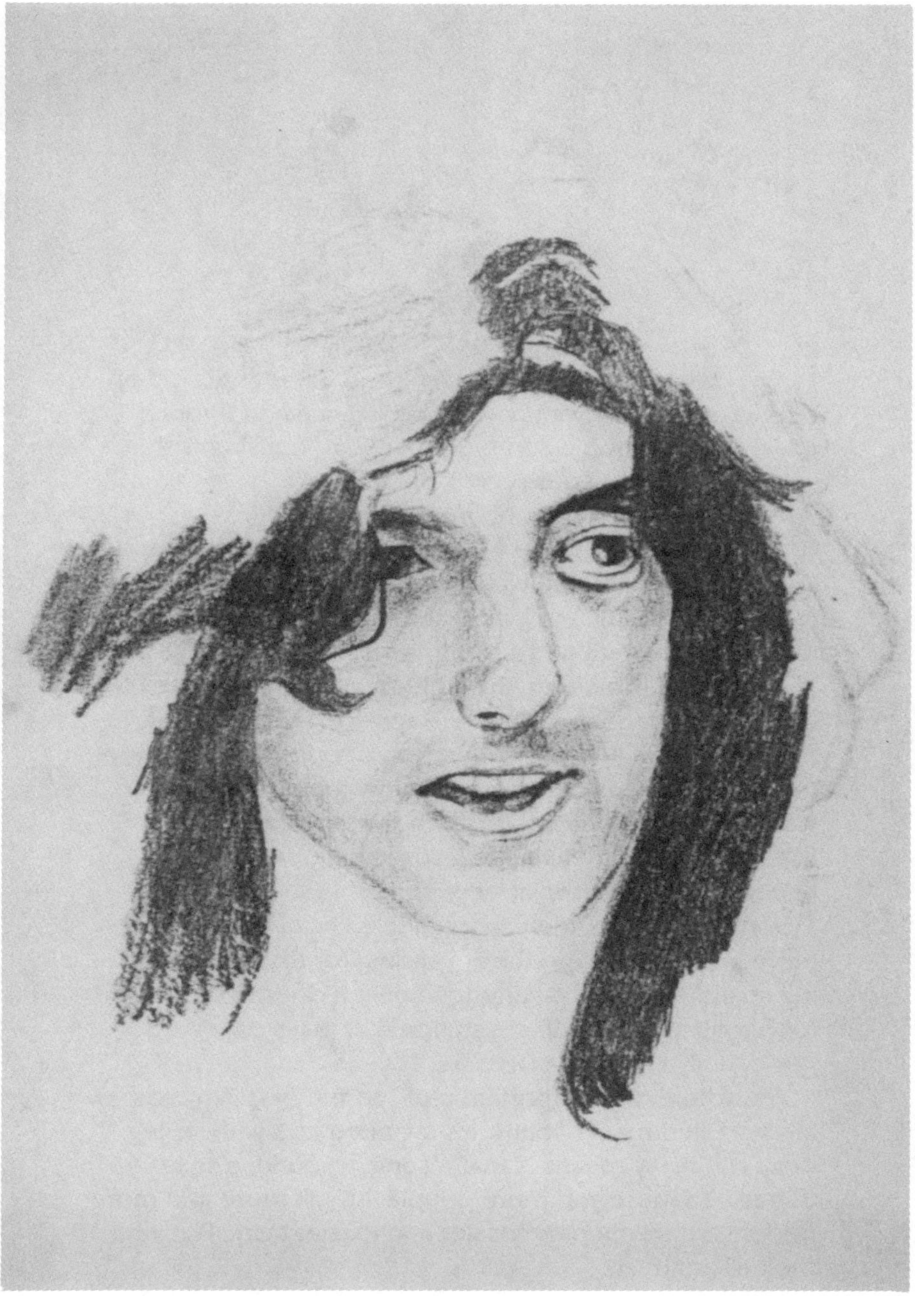

WARNING: THIS CHAPTER CONTAINS BACKWARDS SATANIC MESSAGES

XVIII.
And Rock & Roll

And classical, and jazz, and folk, and blues and... It's all out there, it's now within walking distance and I hope you'll at least sample some of it. College housing is the solution to outrageous record prices.

I could never tolerate obnoxious music critics—"professional" or other—who are into scathing opinions just to sound authoritative. I'm as picky about what I listen to as the next guy, but I can't see arguing about music or just badmouthing bands, albums, musicians, styles.[1] There's a place for everything and too much available to bother with musical snobbery. Raps are great—forcing personal views and preferences on people never did anything for me. Music is one of the few things that offers nothing but enjoyment—no strings attached. It's one of the greatest ice-breakers and something we can all understand—A universal language.

Some music is undeniably infantile. It's planned. It's a business. The garbage they're aiming for that highly profitable and exploitable early-teen bunch doesn't do much for playlist radio. Finding a station that plays only the good stuff is indeed a treasure.

The whole misinterpretation of "commercialism" has always killed me. To many, it's synonymous with selling out. All it really means is that a song, a sound, a style appeals to more and more people. I think more and more people are developing lousier and lousier taste. But who the hell am I?

Music appreciation is not just a gut course. It can be applied on a much more practical level. Knowing what's going on behind the sound enables you to listen **and** hear. You enjoy on a considerably higher level if you choose to. It doesn't mean you have to pick apart every song you listen to and dissect each measure down to the last quarter quaver. But learning about the foundation of anything can't help but make the whole structure more meaningful.

Music history? Rock & Roll: twenty five years and it's treading all over itself. Look at classical music. Now there's timeless stuff. Pop: an endless stream of memories. Blues: pure gut emotion. It's always a reflection of the times. Fascinating stuff. Miss the guitar gods or what? Dinosaurs?...

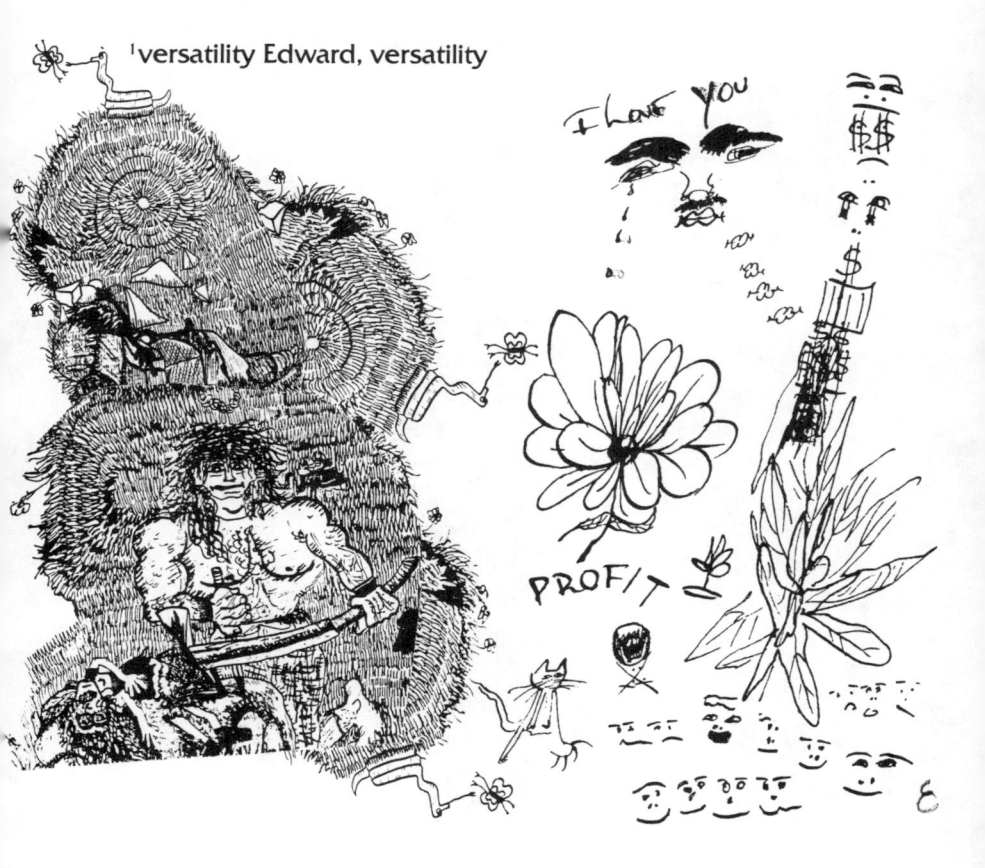

[1] versatility Edward, versatility

I don't want my MTV.

—CB

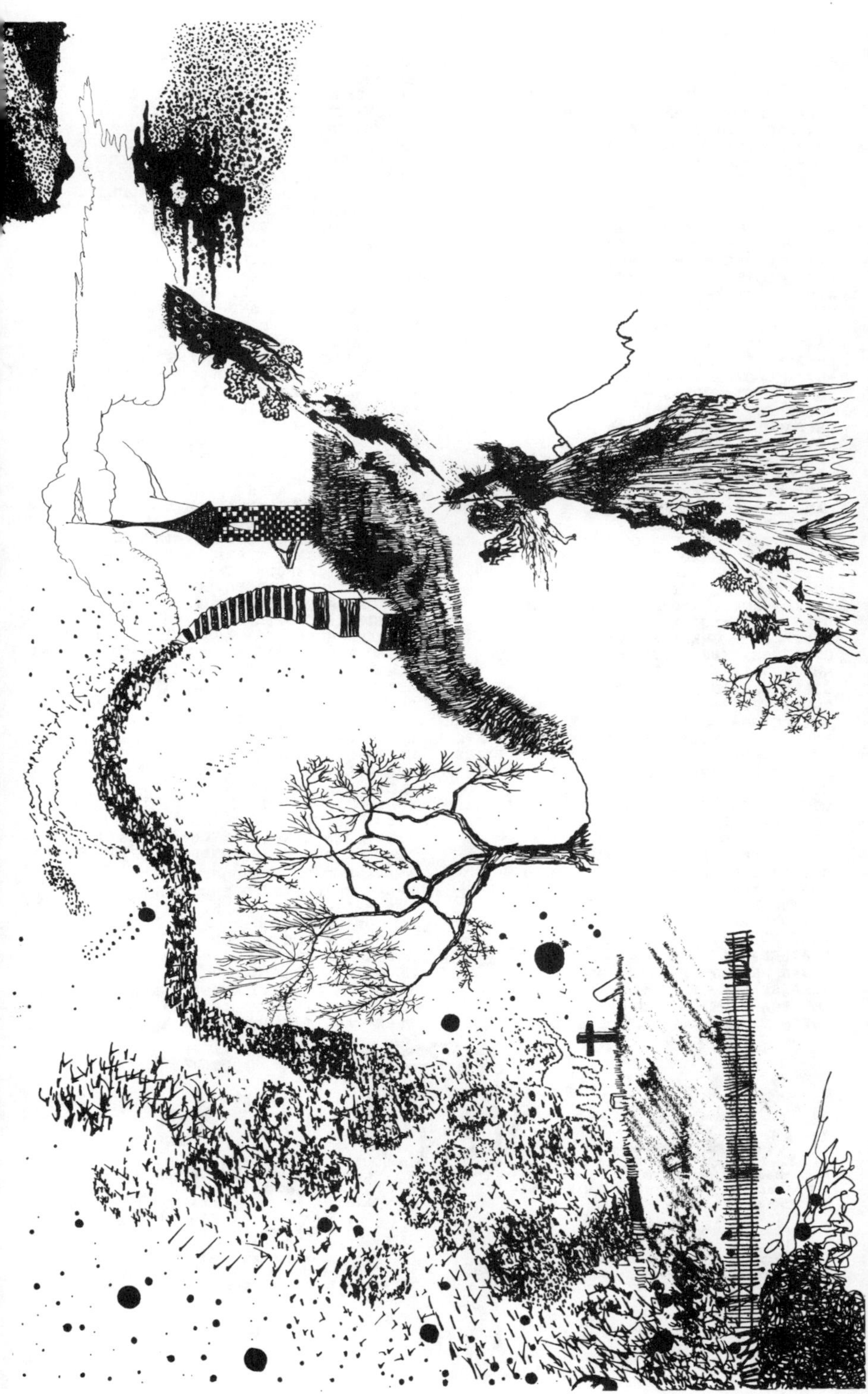

JEFF BECK- TRUTH
JETHRO TULL- MINSTREL IN THE GALLERY
DOOBIE BROS.- THE CAPTAIN AND ME
DAVID GILMOUR- DAVID GILMOUR
ROLLING STONES- EXILE ON MAIN ST.
AL DIMEOLA- ELEGANT GYPSY
DEEP PURPLE- MACHINE HEAD
RICKIE LEE JONES- PIRATES
JOHNNY WINTER- JOHNNY WINTER AND
JOHN FAHEY- BEST OF
ALLMAN BROS.- FILLMORE EAST
MONTROSE- MONTROSE
BLACK SABBATH- PARANOID
YES- CLOSE TO THE EDGE
JIMI HENDRIX- ARE YOU EXPERIENCED
STEVE HILLAGE- FISH RISING
LED ZEPPELIN- PHYSICAL GRAFFITI
JAMES GANG- RIDES AGAIN
HUMBLE PIE- ROCKIN' THE FILLMORE
ALICE COOPER- GREATEST HITS
TOMMY BOLIN- TEASER
SUPREMES- ANTHOLOGY
CHICAGO- CHICAGO II
BILLY JOEL- PIANO MAN
NATIONAL LAMPOON- ANIMAL HOUSE
LITTLE FEAT- WAITING FOR COLOMBUS
PINK FLOYD-]THE WALL[
CAROLE KING- TAPESTRY
LEO KOTTKE- THE BEST
M. BLOOMFIELD- IF YOU LOVE THESE BLUES
ELP-BRAIN SALAD SURGERY
FREDDIE KING- BEST OF
ERIC CLAPTON- HISTORY OF
KINKS- SCHOOL BOYS IN DISGRACE
BTO- NOT FRAGILE
B.B. KING- GREAT MOMENTS
CREDENCE- THE CONCERT
MUDDY WATERS- LIVE
STEVE MARTIN- LET'S GET SMALL
CSN&Y- SO FAR
BOZ SCAGGS- SILK DEGREES
FAIRPORT CONVENTION- FAIRPORT CHRONICLES
TED NUGENT- INTENSITIES IN TEN CITIES
MOTT THE HOOPLE- ALL THE YOUNG DUDES
HEART- DOG AND BUTTERFLY
LOWELL GEORGE- THANKS I'LL EAT IT HERE
JOHN MAYALL w/ E.C.- BLUES BREAKERS
AC/DC-IF YOU WANT BLOOD...
LYNYRD SKYNYRD- SECOND HELPING
STEELY DAN- ROYAL SCAM
DOORS- MORRISON HOTEL
GRATEFUL DEAD- LIVE DEAD
NEIL YOUNG- DECADE
BEATLES- '62-'66
BEATLES- '67-'70
JUDAS PRIEST- BRITISH STEEL
RENAISSANCE- SONG FOR ALL SEASONS
AMERICAN HOT WAX- SOUNDTRACK
ROBIN TROWER- BRIDGE OF SIGHS

VAN HALEN- VAN HALEN II
CHICAGO- GREATEST HITS
JOHN LENNON- JOHN LENNON
POLICE- GHOSTS IN THE MACHINE
PAT METHENY- BRIGHT SIZE LIFE
JOHN MCLAUGHLIN- BELO HORIZONETE
CHUCK BERRY- JUST ABOUT ANYTHING
JIM CROCE- TIME IN A BOTTLE/L.S.
C. ATKINS/L. PAUL- CHESTER & LESTER
BRIAN MAY'S STAR FLEET PROJECT
CREAM- FRESH CREAM
ZZ TOP- TRES HOMBRES
AC/DC- BACK IN BLACK
YES- YESSONGS
BOB DYLAN- HIWAY 61 REVISITED
SON SEALS- LIVE AND BURNING
JANIS JOPLIN- PEARL
JOE COCKER- MAD DOGS & ENGLISHMEN
TODD RUNDGREN- DEFACE THE MUSIC
DIXIE DREGS- NIGHT OF THE LIVING DREGS
BEACH BOYS- ENDLESS SUMMER
SANTANA- CARAVANSERI
AMERICAN GRAFFITI- SOUNDTRACK
ALL. BROS.- THE ROAD GOES ON FOREVER
BRUCE SPRINGSTEEN- THE RIVER
THE DAMNED- STRAWBERRIES
THE BEATLES- ABBEY ROAD
RENAISSANCE- SCHERAZADE & OTHER STORIES
BERT JANSCH- JACK ORION
ROLLING STONES- STICKY FINGERS
GRATEFUL DEAD- TERRAPIN STATION
NATIONAL LAMPOON- THAT'S NOT FUNNY...
JETHRO TULL- WAR CHILD
GEORGE HARRISON- ALL THINGS MUST PASS
ALBERT KING- I'LL PLAY THE BLUES FOR YOU
MICHAEL SCHENKER- ASSAULT ATTACK
EDGAR WINTER- THEY ONLY COME OUT AT NITE
GENE TRACY- TRUCK STOP 4
AEROSMITH- TOYS IN THE ATTIC
SCORPIONS- VIRGIN KILLER
GARY MOORE- CORRIDORS OF POWER
LARRY CARLTON- LARRY CARLTON
NEKTAR- RECYCLED
THE WHO-]QUADROPHENIA[
ALLAN HOLDSWORTH- I.O.U.
CARLY SIMON- TORCH
KISS- ALIVE
ANY ALBUM DANNY KORTCHMAR PLAYS ON
JOHN MCLAUGHLIN- INNER MOUNTING FLAME
STEVE MORSE- INTRODUCTION
UFO- STRANGERS IN THE NIGHT
VAN HALEN- VAN HALEN
ZZ TOP- FANDANGO
YARDBIRDS- LEGEND OF
RODNEY DANGERFIELD- NO RESPECT
MOUNTAIN- BEST OF
SANDY DENNY- WHO KNOWS WHERE THE TIME..
LED ZEPPELIN- LED ZEPPELIN
DEREK AND THE DOMINOES- LAYLA

"Dogs" PINK FLOYD
"Machine Gun" JIMI HENDRIX
"Mean Streets" VAN HALEN
"I'm Yours And I'm Hers" J. WINTER
"Burn" DEEP PURPLE
"Stray Cat Blues" (L) ROLLING STONES
'Fire & Rain' JAMES TAYLOR
"Day Of The Eagle" ROBIN TROWER
"Something" BEATLES

"Love Look What You've Done.." B.SCAGGS
"No Time" GUESS WHO
"Along Came Jones" COASTERS
"One Fine Morning" LIGHTHOUSE
"She's The One" BRUCE SPRINGSTEEN
"Runaway" BONNIE RAITT
"John Barleycorn Must Die" TRAFFIC
"Born Under A Bad Sign" CREAM
'The Battle Of Evermore' LED ZEPPELIN

"Gimme Shelter" (L) GRAND FUNK
'Melissa' ALLMAN BROTHERS
"Where Did Our Love Go" (L) J. GEILS
"Bridge Over Troubled Water" S&G
"When The Levee Breaks" LED ZEPPELIN
"Rockaway Beach" RAMONES
"Love In Vain" ROBERT JOHNSON
"Dance Little Sister" ROLLING STONES
"Trouble In Mind" LIGHTNIN' HOPKINS
"The End" DOORS
'King Of Pain' POLICE
"Juke Box Music" KINKS
"Cross-eyed Mary" (L) JETHRO TULL
"Haven't Got Time For The Pain" C.SIMON
"She Said, She Said" BEATLES
"Monkey Man" ROLLING STONES
"Levon" ELTON JOHN
'Behind Blue Eyes' THE WHO
"You" GEORGE HARRISON
"Northern Lights" RENAISSANCE
"She's So Tough" MINK DEVILLE
"If You Can't Rock Me" (L) ROLLING STONES
"Nobody's Fault" AEROSMITH
"Bad Company" BAD COMPANY
"Celebrate" RARE EARTH
"American Pie" DON MCLEAN
"Misfits" KINKS
"For All We Know" CARPENTERS
"Feelin' Alright" JOE COCKER
"Half Moon" JANIS JOPLIN
"I'm A Man" SPENCER DAVIS
"Shine On You Crazy Diamond' P.FLOYD
"Chestnut Mare" BYRDS
"Tuesday Afternoon" MOODY BLUES
"Hopelessly Devoted" OLIVIA NEWTON JOHN
"Hurts So Bad" LINDA RONDSTADT
"If I Fell" BEATLES
"Reach Out" FOUR TOPS
"Landslide" STEVIE NICKS
"Born To Be Wild" STEPPENWOLF
"Good Lovin'" YOUNG RASCALS
"I Only Want To Be w/ You" D. SPRINGFIELD
"Don't Say You Don't Remember" BEV. BREMMER
"Walk Don't Run" VENTURES
"Never Can Say Goodbye" JACKSON 5
"Diamond Girl" SEALS & CROFTS
"Angel Of The Morning" MERILEE RUSH
"Pleasant Valley Sunday" MONKEES
"Well Respected Man" KINKS
"Ain't Too Proud To Beg" TEMPTATIONS
"Paperback Writer" BEATLES
"..Lost That Lovin' Feeling" RIGHTEOUS BR.
"Charlie Brown" COASTERS
"Bad Time" GRAND FUNK
"Different Drum" STONE PONEYS
"Darkness, Darkness" YOUNGBLOODS
"The Usual" BOB DYLAN
"Hand Of Fate" ROLLING STONES
"Don't Walk Away Renee" LEFT BANK
"I'm Glad You're Here" SUPREMES
"I Feel Fine" BEATLES
"#9 Dream" JOHN LENNON
"House On Pooh Corner" LOGGINS/MESSINA
"She's Got A Way" (L) BILLY JOEL
"Tombstone Shadow" CREDENCE
"Funeral For A Friend" ELTON JOHN
"Gallows Pole" LED ZEPPELIN
"Nobody Does It Better" CARLY SIMON
"Sweet Jane" (L) LOU REED w/ V.U.
"Pinball Wizard/
  See Me, Feel Me" (L) THE WHO
"Surfer Girl" BEACH BOYS
"Do Anything You Wanna Do" EDDIE/H.R.'s
'Gethsemene' J.C. SUPERSTAR
"You Got That Right" LYNYRD SKYNYRD
"Songbird" CHRISTINE MCVIE
"I Got A Name" JIM CROCE
"Rag Doll" FOUR SEASONS
"Talk Of The Town" PRETENDERS
"Sunday Will Never Be The Same" SPANKY/&
"I'd Wait A Million Years" GRASS ROOTS
"Hello, It's Me" TODD RUNDGREN
"Peace Frog" DOORS
"I'm Bad, I'm Nationwide" ZZ TOP
"First Time Ever I Saw Your Face" R. FLACK
"Be My Baby" RONNETTES
"I've Been Lonely Too Long" RASCALS

"We're All Alone" BOZ SCAGGS
"Give Me One More Chance" JACKSON 5
"I'm Losin' You" ROD STEWART
"Over You" UNION GAP
"Desperado" EAGLES
"Buttercup" FOUNDATIONS
"Band Of Gold" FREDA PAYNE
"Don't Pull Your Love" HAMILTON,JOE,ET.AL.
"I Don't Know How To Love Him" E.ELLIMAN
"My Sherie Amour" STEVIE WONDER
"Stormy" VARIOUS ARTISTS
"Along Comes Mary" ASSOCIATION
"Ticket To Ride" BEATLES
"Stawberry Alarm Clock's only hit"
"I Need To Know" TOM PETTY/HEARTBREAKERS
"Last Train To Clarksville" MONKEES
"Baby,Now That I've Found You" FOUNDATIONS
"Every Day's A New Day" SPIRAL STAIRCASE
"Worst That Could Happen" BROOKLYN BRIDGE
"Dock Of The Bay" OTIS REDDING
"Day After Day" BADFINGER
"Kodachrome" PAUL SIMON
"Hard Day's Night" BEATLES
"Maybe, Baby" BUDDY HOLLY
"Puff The Magic Dragon" PETER,PAUL & MARY
"Here Comes The Sun" GEORGE HARRISON
"Seasons Of Wither" AEROSMITH
"Everlasting Love" VARIOUS ARTISTS
"U Don't Have To Say U Love Me" DUSTY S.
"The Song Remains The Same" LED ZEPPELIN
"Ooh, Baby, Baby" LINDA RONDSTADT
"Mack The Knife" BOBBY DARIN
"He's So Fine" CHIFFONS
"Expressway To Your Heart" S. SURVIVORS
"The Way We Were" BARBARA STREISAND
"Vehicle" IDES OF MARCH
"You Make Me So Very Happy" BS& T's
"Woman" GARY PUCKETT/UNION GAP
"Maybe I Know" LESLEY GORE
"Uptight" STEVIE WONDER
"I Saw Her Again" MAMAS & PAPAS
"Happy Just To Dance w/ You" BEATLES
"Who's Sorry Now" CONNIE FRANCIS
"Shadow Dance" WINDHAM HILL SAMPLER
"She's Always A Woman To Me" B. JOEL
"Yesterday" BEATLES
"Please, Please" BEATLES
"She'd Rather Be With Me" TURTLES
"Mr. Bassman" JOHNNY CYMBAL
"My Way" ELVIS PRESLEY
"Honey Child" MARTHA & VANDELLAS
"Baby I Love You" RONNETTES
"Superstar" CARPENTERS
"Dreamboat Annie" HEART
"Achilles Last Stand" LED ZEPPELIN
"Get Ready" TEMPTATIONS
"Long, Long Time" LINDA RONDSTADT
"Break It To Me Gently" BRENDA LEE
"Reflections Of My Life" MARMALADE
"The Game Of Love" WAYNE FONTANA/M.B.
"Positively Four Street" BOB DYLAN
"Hang On Sloopy" McCOYS
"Crazy For You" MADONNA
"Annie's Song" JOHN DENVER
"Heart Breaker" ROLLING STONES
"Whole Lotta Love" LED ZEPPELIN
"Killing Me Softly" ROBERTA FLACK
"Papa's Got A Brand New Bag" J. BROWN
"This Girl Is A Woman Now" G. PUCKETT
"Soldier Boy" SHIRELLES
"To Sir, With Love" LULU
"One Fine Day" CHIFFONS
"Sweet Season" CAROLE KING
"Tiny Dancer" ELTON JOHN
"No Time To Live" JOHNNY WINTER AND
"Tuesday's Gone" (L) LYNYRD SKYNYRD
"Kings & Queens" AEROSMITH
"Must Be Love" JAMES GANG
'Dreamer' TOMMY BOLIN
"Stone Cold Crazy" QUEEN
"Space Station #5" MONTROSE
"Celebration Day" (L) LED ZEPPELIN
"Highway Star" (L) DEEP PURPLE
"Old Man" NEIL YOUNG
"Bell Bottom Blues" DEREK & THE DOMINOES
"Shakin' All Over" (L) THE WHO
'Like A Rolling Stone' BOB DYLAN

H
S T N
 W I
a PUzzle for a KING

spark N store
derive

KEN I

knowledge accompanies legend
but surrenders imagining
keep intentions good
as Merlin evaded
the hooves
the hooves

lhss n lts r'y
lhss n kl tc dn
lgn n kl cnht y f

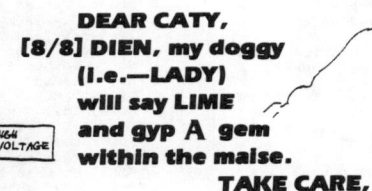

DEAR CATY,
[8/8] DIEN, my doggy
(i.e.—LADY)
will say LIME
and gyp A gem
within the maise.
            TAKE CARE,
                Ed D.

who ll [b] uy ye may lai s aye nyt
whi ye y wil (d'jai s 888 nho L) ai

We can't all be masters
but we can all be composers.

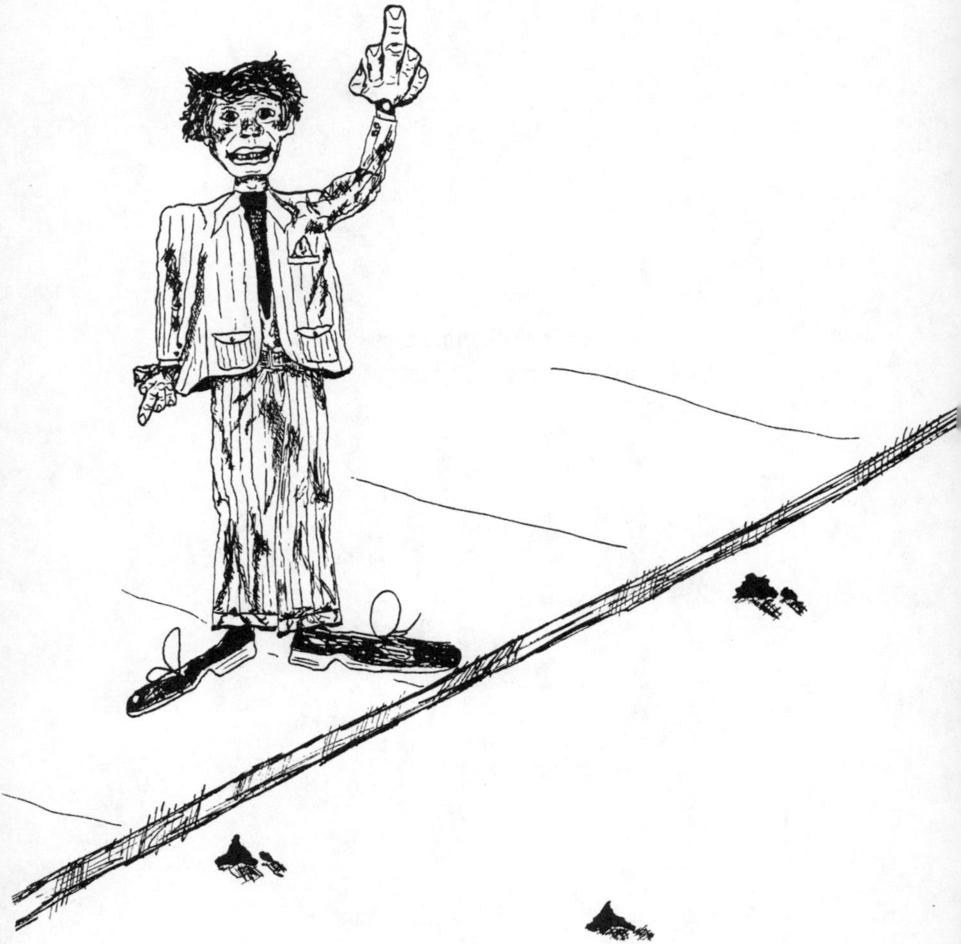

XIX.
Beating The System

Another inappropriately titled chapter. You never really beat the system. You juggle, you improvise, you sleaze by temporarily unscathed. This is nothing to feel guilty about—everybody has to wing it once in a while. You're not always going to have the material down at test time, you're not going to finish every paper on time, you won't have every reading assignment committed to memory and be prepared for discussion on it.

How well you fare in these situations is entirely dependent on three things: 1) Your knowledge of yourself (capabilities, limitations, personality, ability to go without sleep), 2) Your acceptance of the fact that improvising is inevitable and unavoidable and when used judiciously is a valuable personal asset, 3) Your realization that the ability to wing it creatively and productively isn't a gift—it's an acquired skill.

Notes: Recopying them and putting them in order after class is an effective way to commit lecture material to *Notes:* Recopying them and putting them in order after class is an effective way to commit lecture material to memory, but I've never in my life seen anyone do it. Those sketchy outlines that used to work so well for multiple choice tests in highschool are often meaningless when you go back to look at them five weeks later. It might be somewhat painful, but try following the lecture like a conversation and scrawling everything that comes out of prof's mouth right across the page like it's one big sentence. Doing the assigned reading before the corresponding lecture is also surprisingly helpful, but it almost always seems to be the other way around. Technical lectures are torture, but at least making an effort to work through the problems beforehand can't hurt. Slipping a piece of carbon paper under Joe Eigenwave's notes ain't a bad idea either.

Tests. There's not a whole lot of advantage in cheating. Besides defeating the whole educational process, it's an easy way to flunk a course or find yourself outside the college gates. Maybe you'll cheat, but don't rely on it. But sometimes the actual process of making a cheat sheet commits what's on it to memory. This is a well-known phenomenon that probably has some psychological explanation, but who really cares? Right before a test, sit down, think highschool, think small, and write down all pertinent information, formulas, definitions, etc. on a two by two piece of paper. Pay careful attention to detail and convince yourself that you are going to use the thing. Carry it with you to the test and throw it away before you go in. It works.

Papers: Deadlines aren't set in stone. Quality almost always buys extra time after your first paper. If a course requires several papers (English I), do a commendable job on the first one or at least show that you put some effort in. A request for an extension is much more likely to be granted if you can point to a good job on a previous paper. Don't abuse extensions—But if you need them, they're available.

Bozo Work: Just because it's the big leagues doesn't mean that every assignment will be educationally stimulating. Don't labor over obvious worthlessness. Pool your talents, specialize, outline a chapter each, talk things over, weasel stuff from upperclassmen, photo-copy...Be resourceful!

Essay Tests: There's no real substitute for knowing what you're talking about and being able to support it with specific evidence. But generalities can bail you out when you don't have a clue on an essay question. Write everything you know about the topic; use statements that cover all bases and don't commit yourself to anything that

BE THE LEADER

can be totally off the mark. Sometimes, if the rest of your test looks good, a professor will be lenient on a vague, general essay. After four years of taking essay tests at college, you'll be fully trained to write horoscopes.[1]

...In circumstances where the possibility of reducing inflation without a prolonged recession depends heavily on the change of inflationary expectations, there is risk in following a policy many people consider inflationary.*

When you reach this level of professional ambiguity, you'll be fully trained to write economic literature.

I obviously don't know what the hell I'm talking about so I'm not even going to bother wasting your time grading an answer we both know I wrote with a shovel. Minus 10.

Leaving little messages on your test won't necessarily get you more points, but it's something to do while everybody else is busy answering the question and they're a welcome laugh for profs who have to sift through dozens of dry, witless exam answers. Professors appreciate good humor more than you might think and personal messages certainly can't hurt when final grading time rolls around.

Profs: They're people; they're reasonable. They know your bull, but they like to know that you care. Go in and talk to them if you're having academic or personal problems. Don't lie about your situation, but don't be afraid to emphasize desperation. They love a good act.

One semester I was in serious grade trouble and I went in to all my professors right around grading time and told them if I was stuck between two grades, I'd appreciate the higher of the two. I got the higher grade in four out of five courses—the fifth was two grades higher. I did this

SEE ST. PETER

every semester following and boosted an otherwise mediocre GPA to low-grade respectability. Now that I've printed it, it probably won't work anymore.

Finals: Some people start studying for their last one first; others study for their first one first; still others don't even bother studying. It can be a crazy time and nothing I say is going to change that or help much.

When The Going Gets Tough:

Allnighters. They can be surprisingly productive—they can also beat the hell out of you. Test your ability to go without sleep as soon as you can and try not to exceed your limit. Don't rely on waking up a few hours before a test to get the bulk of your studying done. Your mind does some crazy rationalizing during the waking stages and it's relatively easy to talk yourself into rolling over for another five minutes. "I'll just catch five" is usually synonymous with going in unprepared.

Unread Material. You may find yourself preparing for a test and realize that you've got considerably large blocks of material that simply got by you. Maybe worth it at the time, but now it's not looking so great. Read the first paragraph of each chapter and the first and last sentence of paragraphs in between. You'll have a feel for the material in about one-fifth the time it would have taken you to read it carefully. Obviously, you won't know the stuff nearly as well, but desperation is desperation. You could get lucky. For large blocks of unread technical material give up all hope of absorbing anything substantial. Prayer, dropping the course, changing your major—They're all viable alternatives.

Writing at the typewriter. You'd be amazed at how fast the gears spin when you're under pressure. I've done almost this whole chapter off the cuff and the only thing I screwed up was forgetting to mention the footnote and bibliography pages under the "Papers" section. They can take almost as long as the entire rest of your paper and by the time you get to them you are usually mentally incompetent to deal with mosquitoes—much less proper format.

[1]X!
*taken from a 1982 government economic report

Footnotes

(1) A book by a single author:
   [14]Willie Twipples, **Landing The Big One: Job Hunting Made Easy** (Bullet City, Iowa: Pumpkinhead Press, 1982), p. 24.

(2) A book by a single author:
   [8]Joe Kalhoon and Joseph Phallin, **Turn Any Room Into a Stud Palace** (Fort Lauderdale, Florida: Ballbuster Books, 1983), p.43.

(3) A book that is part of a series:
   [16]Bobby Toungeford, **Leadership, Discipline And Strategy.** The Pigmaster Chronicles, No. 5 (Macon, Bayken: Balloonhead Books, 1984), p. 75.

(4) An article from an encyclopedia:
   [10]"Augie Dog," **Ramblin' House Encyclopedia,** 1979, XII, p.72.

(5) An article in a newspaper:
   [15]M. Link, "Who Said The Cavemen Are Dead?," **Pillaging Times,** 26 May 1982, p. 4.

(6) An article in a magazine:
   [7]Herm L. Skinhead, "Home, Jerome," **Mishu Review,** 21 November 1981, p. 58.

(7) Secondary Footnotes:
   [26]Twipples, p.20.

Bibliography

(1) A book by a single author:
   Drayer, Luke. **Who Needs Underwear?** Beach Haven, NJ: Bench Press, 1996.

(2) A book by more than one author:
   Brown, E. and B. Lockhead. **Carpeting Ceramic Tile With Dirty Underwear For Fun And Profit.** Smuggler's Notch, Bahamas: Forward Drink Books, 1981.

(3) A book that is part of a series:
   Toh, Kay. **Nothing From Columns A or B.** Care And Feeding Of The Intramural Wrestler, No. 3. Wahjah, Tokyo: Beaners Books, 1941.

(4) An article from an encyclopedia:
   "Laffer Curve." **Joan The Moan Encyclopedia of Economics.** 1979, VI, 445-6.

(5) An article in a newspaper:
   Estes, T. "Reflections On A Decade Of Higher Education." **Dinknut Daily News,** 27 May 1983, p. 1,8.

(6) An article in a magazine:
   Noxious, Bob. "What Does A Cowboy Hat And A Hemroid Have In Common?" **Droopy Dog Digest,** 30 Ray 1982, p. 789.

This section took nearly two hours and I wish you could have seen all the mistakes. Obviously, this isn't a comprehensive guide. A good English handbook is a worthwhile investment.

Going into tests totally cold. As a last resort, testing memory retention and improvising potential can be very educational, but not everyone has such total disregard for their GPA.

Rice Krispies say "Snap! Crackle! Pop!"
only in English-speaking countries. In
Sweden, the cereal says "Piff! Paff! Puff!"
In South Africa, it's "Knap! Knaetter! Knak!"
and in Germany, "Knisper! Knasper! Knusper!"

—SM

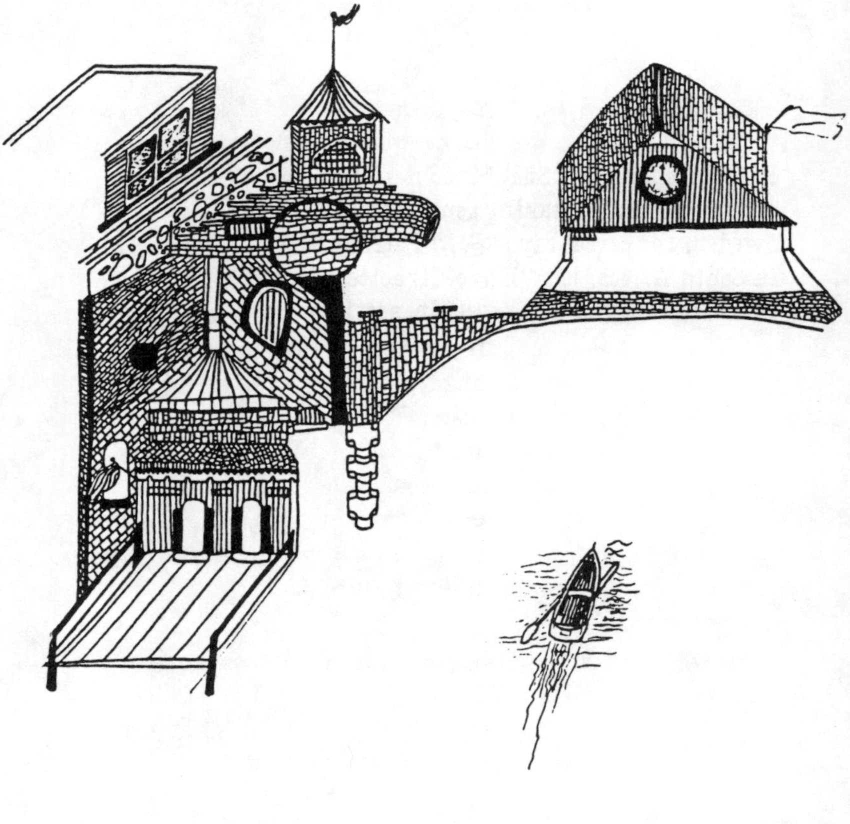

XX.
Door Prizes

   Miscellaneous chapters are usually an author's blatant admission that he screwed up and left stuff out. Personally, I just couldn't figure out how to fit these in before. Treat them like P.S.'s on a letter. They are by no means comprehensive definitions or explanations; some are mildly humorous, others are thoroughly useless, but a few are uselessly thorough. All are less usely rough, though.

Attendance—Some professors are sticklers; others couldn't care less. Find out early who's who and act accordingly.

Sicknesses—They're a lot like flies. They always come at the wrong time; they never seem to go away and they have no real value. Take care of yourself! In the next four years you are going to lead a lifestyle centered around total body abuse. Watch your eating habits. Junk food, outside of being nutritionally worthless and a prime cause of the freshman fifteen, is a major contributor to poor health. Sugar diseases are running rampant, the effects are not pleasant and people are failing to make the connection. Fight sickness in bed. In the long-run, you'll be better off dropping everything and knocking a bug out of you in a few days, rather than trying to function at half-speed for a few weeks.

Cocktail Parties—Barbie and Ken play dress-up in a relaxed atmosphere of booze, snacks and idle chit-chat. Usually held as post-game celebrations. Girls have to leave at half-time to start getting ready for them, but the resulting fashion show is well worth it. Guys look almost human for a few hours.

Holidays—It's easy to forget them—Try not to. A string of lights, a branch with some tinsel wrapped around it, a snowball fight, a card home. They only come once a year.

Advisor—More than a guidance counselor—Pick his

EL PASSO

brains. Your first one might have as few clues as you do, so be wary. Once you settle on a major, you'll get one who usually knows what he's talking about.

Oral Presentations—Excessive and needless verbocity is superfluous and ultimately leads to banality, redundance, plethora, glut, nimiety, scar raps, intemperance and poor grades.

Freshman—A quick moving but clumsy critter with a lot to learn and plenty of time and opportunities to do so.

Home Sweet Home Sweet Home—College or your house? Visitor? If you make it that way. You'll be changing at a much more rapid pace than your folks, but you can't expect everything to change around you. Take your college rules home and you will be treated like a visitor. Appreciate your roots and home will always be your house.

Scabs—Wounded veal facsimiles

Weekend Meals—Not all schools poison you on the weekends. Some do for a year, then let you hunt for your chow. Popping around the various pizza houses, delis, snatch bars and fast-food joints with the knuckleheads was always entertaining, never filling, and a constant drain on the wallet. Plan Ahead!

Good Moderately Priced Champagne—Taylor, Great Western

Sophomore—A more introspective beast that slowly begins to develop a direction, but still has little or nothing to worry about.

Cooperation—Doing with a smile, things you have to do anyway.

Weather—Wind blows.

Chew—All it takes is a pinch between your cheek and gum to look either very laid-back or very ridiculous. The taste and effects are definitely acquired, but it does something for you that can't quite be put into words. Knocking over chew cups is the easiest route to unpopularity.

EL CRASHO

College Newspaper Editorial Section—Anything that can be complained about will be complained about.

Wombats—Harmless groundskeepers who catch a lot of shit for keeping the Magic Kingdom looking nice.

Vandalism—S.low O.n the B.ottle E.njoy the R.oam

Junior—Essentially a vice-presidential knucklehead with all the benefits of Senior, but without the headache of not having a job.

Major—A course concentration, a way of filing you, and a space on your diploma. Usually nothing more.

Government, Law—Everything you always wanted to know—you will argue about instead.

English—Everything you always wanted to know will take you forever to completely dissect.

Psychology—Everything you always wanted to know about anything is usually fascinating.

Pre-Med—Everything you always wanted to know—you must.

Economics—Everything you couldn't care less about knowing can be made into a chart or graph.

Business—Everything you always knew all along now has a label or can be put into a list.

Engineering—Everything you always wanted to know about anything is beyond your comprehension.

Philosophy—Everything you always wanted to know about anything—you can only contemplate.

History—Everything you always wanted to know about anything.

Computer Science—Anything and everything you always wanted to know—it can do faster and more efficiently.

Education—Everything you always wanted to know about anything is all around you.

Music—A creative foreign language

Religion—Could Christie Brinkley have evolved from an ape?

Hangover Remedies—Anything that gets the blood pumping through your system and increases oxygen intake—Ultimate Frisbee, funnelating, getting big, blind dates, beaver shooting.

Beards—A sock for the face and less surface area for zits to migrate to.

Seminar Rooms—It is not better to remain silent and be judged a fool, than to speak and remove all doubt.

Vandalism—S.ave O.n B.ailbonds E.nroll at R.iker's

Sleep—When you can't; get out of bed as soon as you realize that you're not drowsy. Do something—anything—till you feel tired. Then go back to bed. Condition your mind into remembering that your bed really is a place to sleep. (feye)

Hierarchy of Poker Hands—Royal Flush...Straight Flush.-..Four of a Kind...Full House...Flush...Straight...Three of a Kind...Two Pair...Pair...Fold.

Hierarchy of Backgammon—checkers with dice...chess with dice...procrastination device...dust collector.

Pigmania—Perhaps the greatest parlor game of our time. The rules never seem to sink in, but somebody always knows them. Powerchowing is the only rule everyone is familiar with.

Vandalism—S.top O.ffenders B.uy E.xploding R.eplicas

Why I Hate Some Textbooks—"Should modernization cease to proliferate, the prognostications are not entirely gloomy."

How That Could Have Been Said—It won't be all that bad if technology doesn't continue to improve.

An Actual Equation In An Engineering Textbook—

$$G(jw) = \frac{K_b \Pi\Pi_{i=1}^{Q}(1+jwTi)}{(jw)^N \Pi\Pi_{n=1}^{M}(1+jwT_n) \Pi\Pi_{k=1}^{R}[1+(2L_k/w_{n_k})jw + (jw/w_{n_k})^2]}$$

AHEAD WARP 7

Grimpus' Law—Don't put off till tomorrow what you can put off till next week or next month.

Grimpus' Corollary—Don't put off till tomorrow what you can put off till next week or next month or not do at all.

Jim's Spontaneous Theory of Forgotten Insight—

Amish Proverb—Too soon old, too late smart.

Shroomish Proverb—If the shit fits, wear it.

Jim's Theory of Spontaneous Forgotten Insight—If it was any good, it's been said before or it'll be said again.

Joe's Attempt At A Law—Don't blow it, if you can blow it off.

Practical Advice From W.C. Fields—Always carry a flagon of whiskey in case of snakebite, and furthermore always carry a small snake.

General Obvious Comment—Ninety-nine percent of intelligence is being intelligent at the right time.

Senior—A fun-loving knucklehead with one eye on the future, another on the past and the ability to do anything he wants.

EDITH KEELER MUST DIE

No man has the right to arrogate
to himself one particle of superiority
or consideration because he has
had a college education, but it
makes it doubly incumbent upon him
to do well and nobly in his life.

—TR

Why then, the world's mine oyster which I with sword will open.

—S

If you wish to know the road up the mountain,
ask the person who goes back and forth on it.

—Z

Our's is a world where people don't know what they want
and are willing to go through anything to get it.

—DM

Success is a journey, not a destination.

—BS

Knowledge is good.

—MF

In making a living today, many
no longer leave room for life.

—JRS

It's a game of resilience, day in and day out.

—TM

It must be borne in mind that
the tragedy in life doesn't
lie in not reaching your goal.
The tragedy lies in having no
goal to reach. It isn't a
calamity to die with dreams
unfulfilled, but it is a calamity
not to dream. It is not a disaster
to be unable to capture your ideal,
but it is a disaster to have no
ideal to capture. It is not a disgrace
not to reach the stars, but it is
a disgrace to have no stars to
reach for. Not failure, but low
aim is sin.

—BM

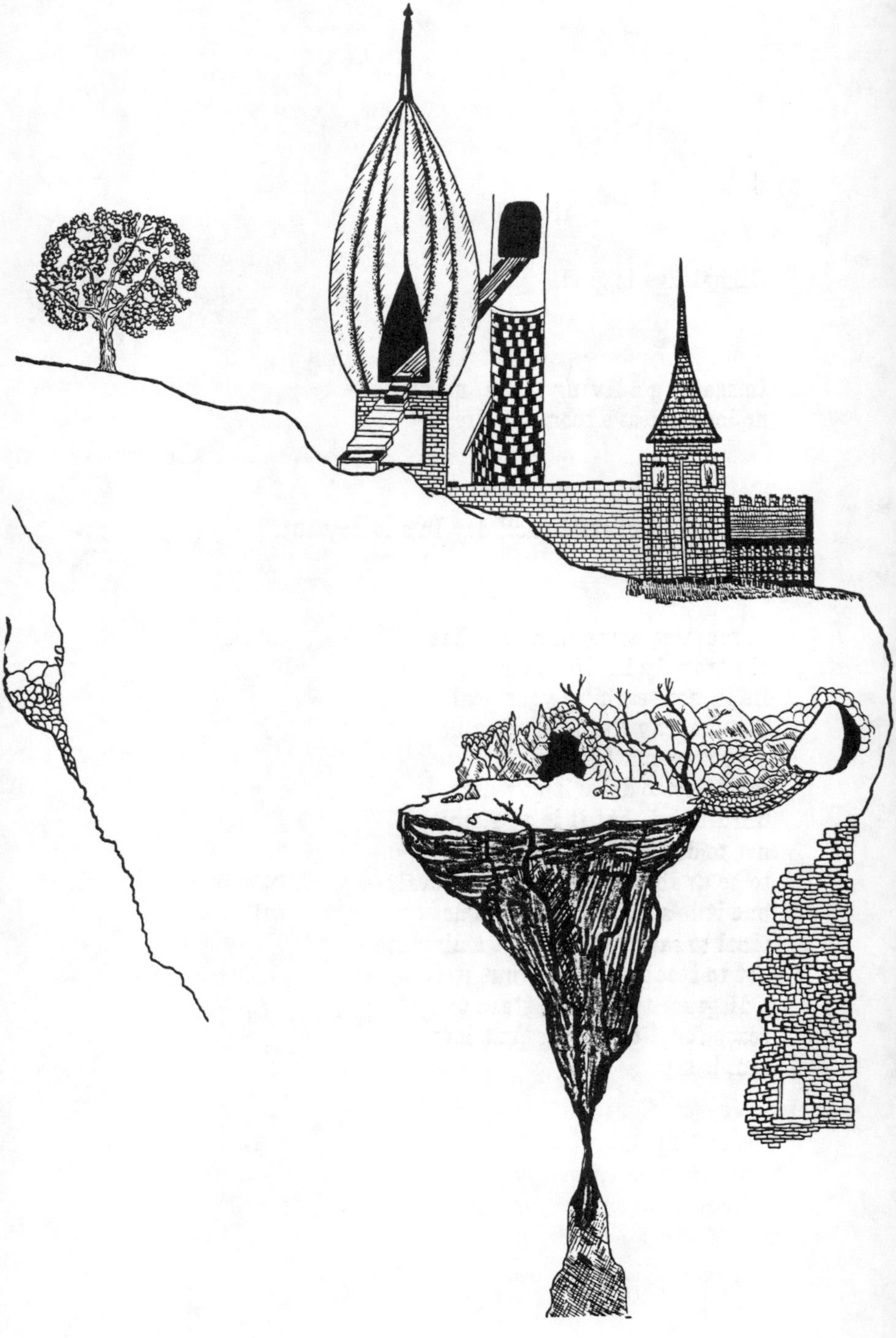

XXI.
After...

Four years? A blink of an eye. You thought highschool whipped by? You'll be in and out of here faster than you can kick a pony keg. But oh, the time spent...

College makes no guarantees to turn you into a mental monster. The initiative always starts from within. But if you come in with any kind of head on your shoulders, a desire to learn, and a sense of humor, you'll leave a person with considerably more clues than when you arrived.

College can't be put into a box. It's so many things to so many people and individuality always rules. I like to think that I've presented a pretty good picture, but I never promised the whole story. You make your circumstances what you want them to be. I think that's the underlying principle behind the whole deal. You gradually become smart enough to influence your environment—to shape it to fit your desires, to fit the desires of others, to change what you don't like, to adapt to what can't be changed, to show others how to make **their** environment better, to always keep yourself entertained, productive and fulfilled.

I'm not crazy about being thought of as typical, but I guess in a lot of ways I'm just an average sort of knucklehead. I share the same thoughts and feelings as everybody else—Probably nobody has bothered to make such a science of inquisition, but then nobody's tried to document all this before. This book was more than just noticing things—It was making a real effort to learn about and from everything and everyone I came into contact with.

It's such a great gift that we are all naturally able to teach one and other—whether we realize it or not. Enjoy everybody; go after people; don't give up on anyone without putting some time and effort in. Good instruction isn't always cheap or easy.

You're always learning about yourself. Some people scoff at the idea of "finding yourself at college." We're here to slave, sweat and get a job. Don't buy it. If you were selling a product, you'd find out everything you could about it—What it can do, what it can't do, what it shouldn't do, who can use it best, etc. You're always selling yourself.

I'm glad you read this because teaching is my first love. Put it down and read it again sometimes during your four years. Getting you while you are still a seed or, at least impressionable, is the key to learning. Real appreciation comes when you've grown.

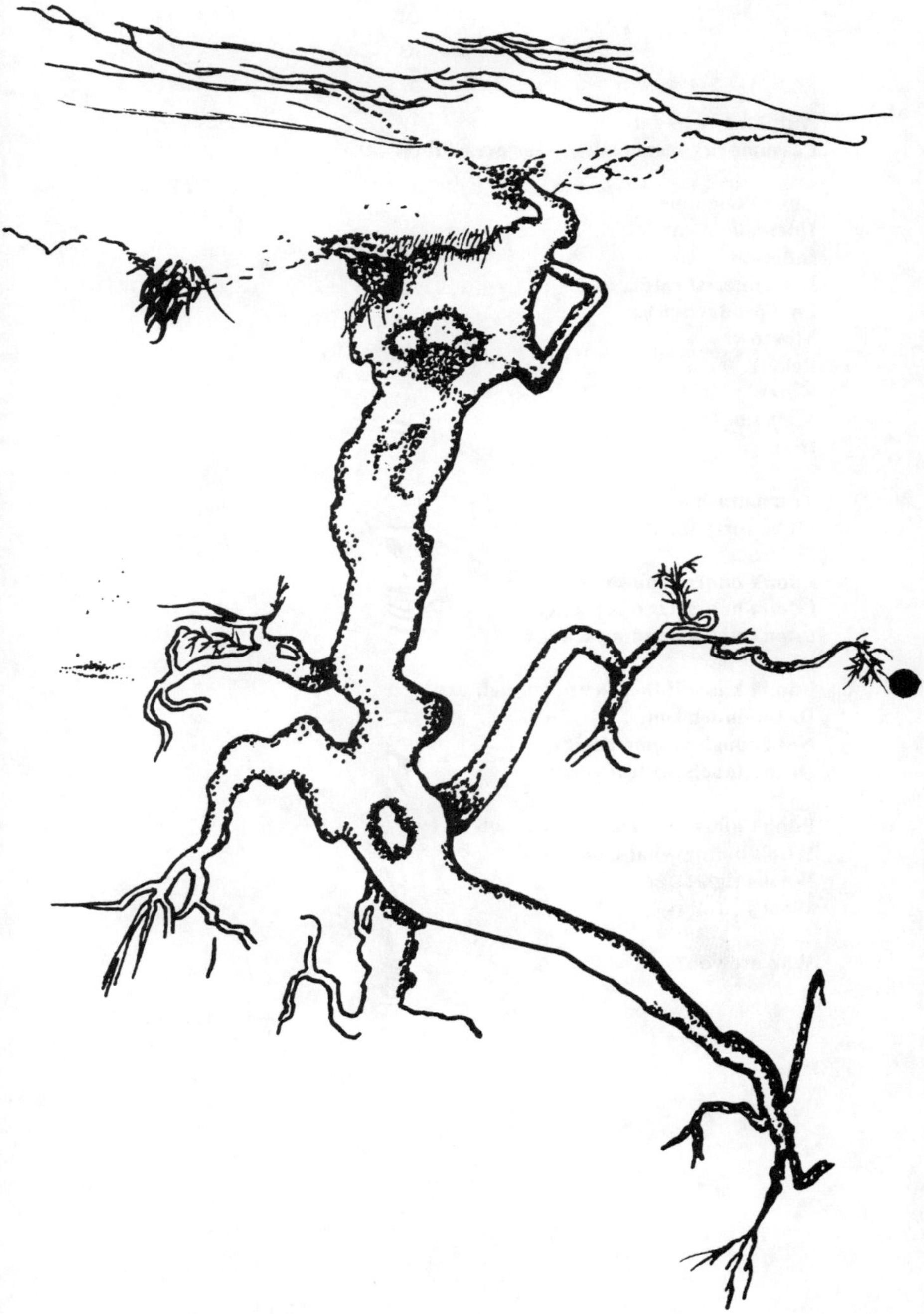

Alright, I've had it.
I assume full responsibility for everything.

Cheryl Gibbons.
Unemployment.
Inflation.
High interest rates.
Low productivity.
Moscow.
Peking.
Korea.
Vietnam.
Iran.

You name it—
I'll be sorry for it.

I don't understand my son,
I don't understand my wife.
I don't understand myself.

I don't know if there's not enough gas;
Or too much sun.
Not enough atomic energy;
Or too much nuclear waste.

I don't know if there's not enough love;
Who's hiding what from who;
What's right;
What's wrong—

Who are you?

—George Duppler

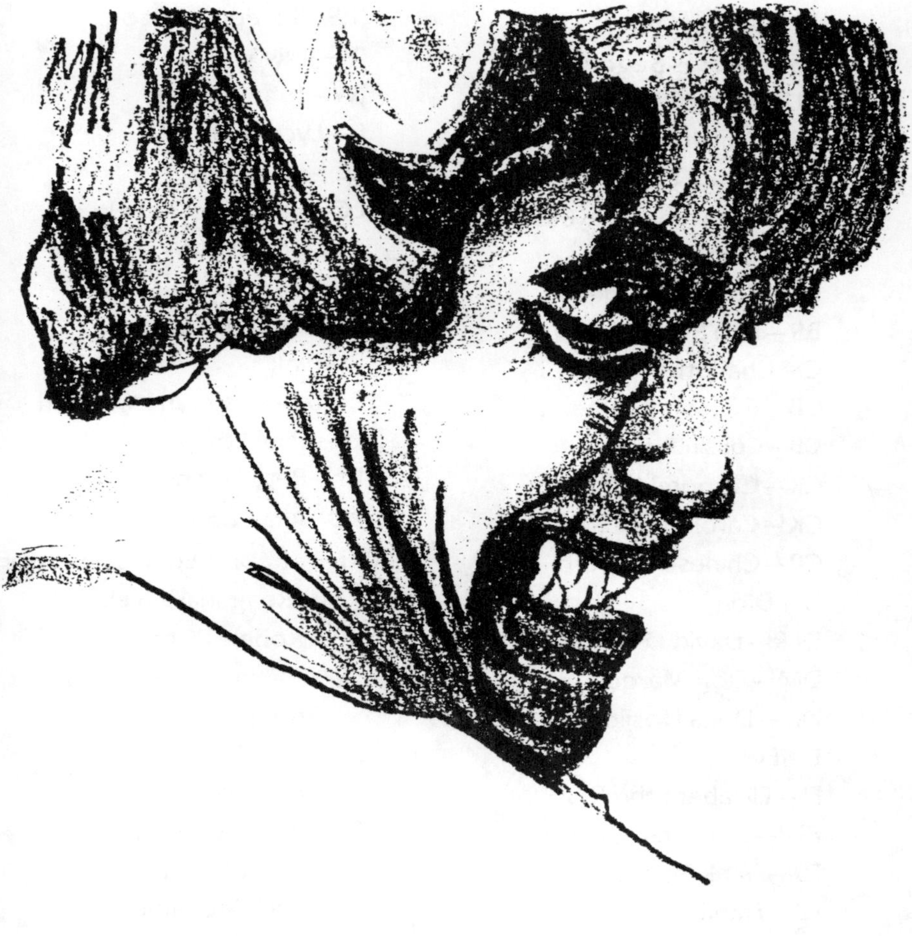

A — Adam
AC — Alice Cooper
AH — Alduous Huxley
AE — Albert Einstein
ARP — Army Recruitment Poster
AS — Adam Smith
AS — Andres Segovia
AU — Author Unknown
BB — Buffalo Bill
BC — Butch Cassidy
BM — Benjamin Mayes
BO — Benjamin Orr
BS — Bumper Sticker
BS — Ben Sweetland
C — Charlotte
CB — Captain Beefheart
CB — Cousin Brucie
CK — Corporal Klinger
CK — Carol King
CP — Chinese Proverb
D — Dion
DLR — David Lee Roth
DM — Don Marquis
DU — Delta Upsilon
E — Eve
EI — Elizabeth the First
ETP — Evan Trans. Paystub
FS — Frank Serpico
FZ — Frank Zappa
GDI — Gizmo Development, Inc.
GP — Grandmother Pryor
GR — Giovanni Ruffini
HDT — Henry David Thoreau
HS — Humane Scty.

JB — John Buchan
JD — John Dewey
JH — Johnny Hooker
JM — Joni Mitchell
JP — Joe Phi '27
JRS — Joseph R. Sizoo
JV — Jolly Vilano
JW — John Walker
L — Lycurgus
LC — Lewis Caroll
LC — Lord Chesterfield
LT — Lily Tomlin
MF — Mr. Faber
ML — Martin Luther
P — Pink
PIMR — poster in my room
PL — Paul Lowney
PT — Pete Townsend
RC — Rita Coolidge
RLS — Robert Louis Stevenson
RM — Reagan McNeil
RP — Robert Plant
RWE — Ralph Waldo Emerson
S — Snoopy
S — Squealer
S — Shakespeare
SC — Steve Carlton
SM — Scot Morris
TM — Tim McCarver
TR — Teddy Roosevelt
VC — Vito Corleone
WMT — William Makepeace Thackeray
Z — Zenrin

Artwork: Robert Michael Clemenza

Typesetting: Wyckoff Graphic Arts

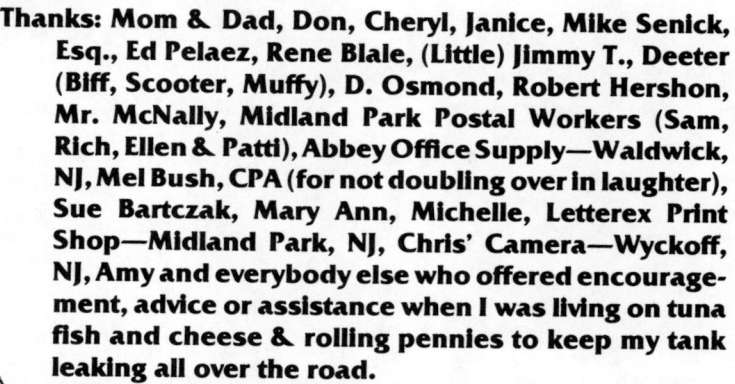

Thanks: Mom & Dad, Don, Cheryl, Janice, Mike Senick, Esq., Ed Pelaez, Rene Blale, (Little) Jimmy T., Deeter (Biff, Scooter, Muffy), D. Osmond, Robert Hershon, Mr. McNally, Midland Park Postal Workers (Sam, Rich, Ellen & Patti), Abbey Office Supply—Waldwick, NJ, Mel Bush, CPA (for not doubling over in laughter), Sue Bartczak, Mary Ann, Michelle, Letterex Print Shop—Midland Park, NJ, Chris' Camera—Wyckoff, NJ, Amy and everybody else who offered encouragement, advice or assistance when I was living on tuna fish and cheese & rolling pennies to keep my tank leaking all over the road.

Also, thanks to David Saltman, Graphic Arts Consultant, who I've never met but who somehow managed to add an intangible to this book that wasn't there a few months ago.

Thanks to John Baumgartner for help with seventh generation revisions and improvements.

Special thanks to Jim Philbrick without whom, etc.

Shots: Shoody, Squirman, J. Daniels, Blimple (Hoagie Slayer)

Tune sheet typeset for mice by the author on an IBM PC

Style Pointers, General Guidance:
Profs. Bradford and Piper

In Memory...

Kevin Anthony Clemenza
March 5, 1956-December 10, 1982

Life is the childhood of our immortality.

—**Goethe**

SHREWD, AWARE, INTELLIGENT INDIVIDUALS WHO BEAT THE LINES AND
PLACED ADVANCE ORDERS FOR THIS BOOK.

DIANE BOYLE	BOB SOTTILE	JAMES B. AVINO
KIM KNAPP	PAT FORAY	JIM & GAIL TURNER
JOHN DEVINE	MRS. ADDIS	JAKE BLUES
MARK MULHOLLAND	MIKE NASSOR	NEIL GALLIGAN
MARIA WIESEHAHN	JEANNETTE REEVES	FRAN MOFFA
PHIL CINELLI	BILL BURKE	MISS HARLOWE
DEAN SOTTILE	KIM CORNELL	KAREN MASSAMINO
KATHY FIERY	BARBARA HEIMSTRA	DAVE GUILLOD
ROB MICHEL	SABINA REICHARDT	TOM ESTES
DAVE TURNER	BILL HOBAN	AL COGNIGNI
TODD WILSON	HEIDI BUKLER	ACITO FAMILY
WAYNE MYERS	LARRY GRIFFIN	MARIANNE GRAY
BOB & KATHY CLARK	RALPH HOLMES	KATHY BEARD
ED VORE	DOUG JACKSON	BILL CASEY
GEOF MULFORD	AMY MORRIS	KATHY VAN HOOK
ELLIE	VOLPE FAMILY	LISA KADIN
TIM MCANDREW	DAVE BRADY	CYNTHIA VERDONE
JOHN XANTHOPOULOS	TOM GIOIA	MARK BALZARETTE
BRIAN GITKIN	JEFF LIST	BEN RAETZ

<<<<<<<<<<<<<<<<<<<<<<<<<<<<<<<<<<<<<<<<<<<<<<<<<<<<<<<<<<
FOR ALL YOUR BUSINESS, CREATIVE, ENTERTAINMENT & BASIC NEEDS...
>>

ACCEL COURIER SYSTEMS-- THE SERVICE ACE -- WALDWICK, NJ
-- (800) 83-ACCEL --   -- (201) 652-4900 --

TOM GIOIA-- HIGH TECH GUITAR INSTRUCTION --
"Learn Musicianship Through Music"
-- (201) 941-2281 --

LEVEL THREE PRODUCTIONS-- AUDIO PRODUCTION -- LEWISTOWN, PA
"We Do The Fun Stuff First"
-- (717) 248-9836 --

GRIMPUS BOOKING AGENCY
PERSONALIZED LIVE ENTERTAINMENT FOR ANY OCCASION
!!
SMALL AND LARGE PARTIES, FRATERNITY WEEKENDS, OPEN AIR SHOWS
!!

*****ROCK, FOLK, BLUES, CLASSICAL GUITAR--ANY OR ALL*****
WE TAKE CARE OF EVERYTHING!
Extensive Experience in Tailoring a Show to Fit Your Needs
VERY REASONABLE RATES
JIM GREY   -- (201) 891-4162 --

FRANK SCHOOFS-- INDEPENDENT FILM MAKER -- GLEN ROCK, NJ
-- (201) 447-4513 --

ED & ROSEMARY-- ADVERTISING/COPYWRITING -- (201) 791-4610

MIKE NASSOR-- DRUM LESSONS/ ALL LEVELS -- WYCKOFF, NJ
-- (201) 891-5680 --

JIM GREY-- GUITAR LESSONS -- WYCKOFF, NJ
"When You're Not Quite Ready For Tom Gioia"
-- (201) 891-4162 --

MARK J. BALZARETTE STUDIOS-- COMMERCIAL PHOTOGRAPHY --
WALDWICK,NJ   -- (201) 652-4678 --

EVAN TRANSPORTATION-- PERSONALIZED TRANSPORTATION SERVICES --
School & Team Charters
OAKLAND, NJ   -- (201) 337-6400 --

ACKERMAN'S MUSIC CENTER-- SCHOOL OF MUSIC, INSTRUMENTS,
ACCESSORIES, REPAIRS, REHEARSAL STUDIOS
Where Courteous Professional Service Is An Artform
MIDLAND PARK, NJ
ANTHONY J. AMMIRATO   -- (201) 444-4955 --

RANCH DINER-- "A FAMILY RESTAURANT WHERE FRIENDS MEET AN EAT" --
BRANCHBURG, NJ   -- (201) 526-4040 --

ABOUT BOOKS, INC.-- AMERICA'S PREMIER FULL SERVICE WRITING,
PUBLISHING, AND BOOK MARKETING FIRM --
BOX 538-B, COUNTY RD. ff38, SAGUACHE, CO 81149
-- (719) 589-5995 --

BOOK MASTERS-- TOTAL BOOK PUBLISHING SERVICES --
-- NEW COMPUTER CONTROLLED CASEBINDING LINE FOR GREATER ECONOMY
FOR SHORTER RUNS--
"We're Professionals With A Personal Touch"
-- (800) 537-6727 --

CARTER & ASSOCIATES-- CREATIVE MARKETING STRATEGIES --ARDMORE, PA
-- (215) 649-3051 --

KMK COURIER-- SAME DAY DELIVERY SERVICE -- FRANKLIN LAKES, NJ
-- (201) 891-4790 --

MOUNTAIN PRINTING AND COPY CENTER-- WALDWICK, NJ
"A New Concept in Full Service"
-- (201) 447-6627 --

BRIAN GITKIN-- GUITARIST -- FRANKLIN LAKES, NJ -- (201) 891-7743

JEFF LIST-- SINGER -- WYCKOFF, NJ -- (201) 891-8721 --

BEN RAETZ-- GUITARIST -- RIDGEWOOD, NJ -- (201) 444-7196 --

IDEAL SOUND-- REHEARSAL STUDIOS -- HACKENSACK, NJ
-- (201) 488-7060 --

FRANK'S RECORDS-- NEW, USED & RARE RECORDS BOUGHT AND SOLD --
RIVER EDGE, NJ   -- (201) 967-8273 --

BRIDGEWATER COPY & PRINT-- BRIDGEWATER, NJ -- (201) 231-8585 --

DORENE'S DELI-- CATERING -- SOMERVILLE, NJ -- (201) 534-2225 --

THE PRINT CENTER-- A NON-PROFIT ORGANIZATION PROVIDING THE FULL
RANGE OF PRE-PRODUCTION AND PRODUCTION SERVICES FOR SMALL
PRESSES AND PUBLISHERS OF BOOKS, MAGAZINES AND NEWSLETTERS --
-- (212) 206-8465 --

R & J FENCE CO.-- CHAIN LINK AND WOOD FENCING --
BERGENFIELD, NJ
Free Estimates / Fully Insured
-- (201) 384-3556 --

OUTERBRIDGE CROSSING-- ORIGINAL HARD ROCK --
for booking call
(201) 567-5638   OR   (201) 891-4162

CUSTOM RACK
DESIGN
****
Personalized Amplification Systems For The Discerning Guitarist
****
TOM GIOIA   -- (201) 941-2281 --

WYCKOFF GRAPHIC ARTS
ONE STOP->>>>>>>DESIGN/TYPE/PRINTING/PHOTOGRAPHY -- WYCKOFF, NJ
-- (201) 891-2222 --

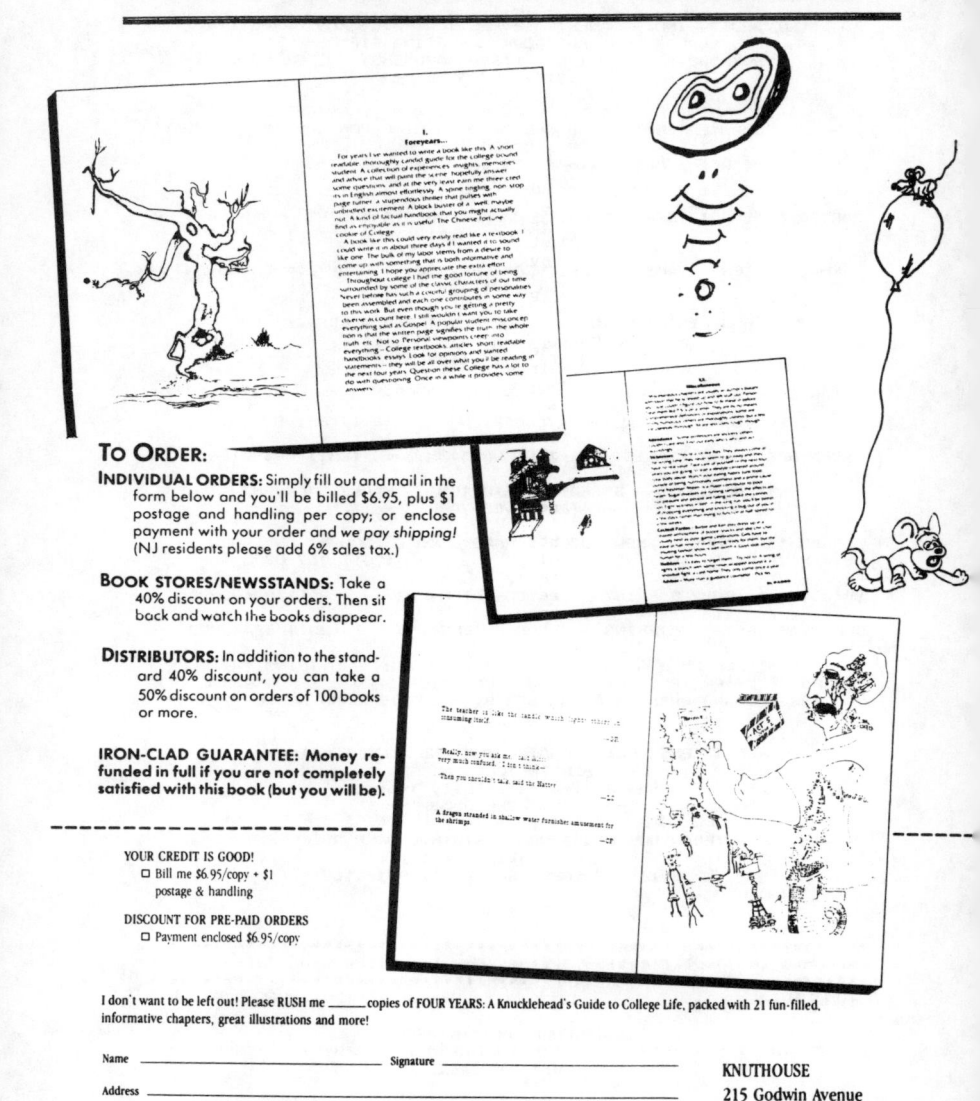

Four Years
A Knucklehead's Guide To College Life

TO ORDER:

INDIVIDUAL ORDERS: Simply fill out and mail in the form below and you'll be billed $6.95, plus $1 postage and handling per copy; or enclose payment with your order and we pay *shipping!* (NJ residents please add 6% sales tax.)

BOOK STORES/NEWSSTANDS: Take a 40% discount on your orders. Then sit back and watch the books disappear.

DISTRIBUTORS: In addition to the standard 40% discount, you can take a 50% discount on orders of 100 books or more.

IRON-CLAD GUARANTEE: Money refunded in full if you are not completely satisfied with this book (but you will be).

YOUR CREDIT IS GOOD!
☐ Bill me $6.95/copy + $1 postage & handling

DISCOUNT FOR PRE-PAID ORDERS
☐ Payment enclosed $6.95/copy

I don't want to be left out! Please RUSH me _____ copies of FOUR YEARS: A Knucklehead's Guide to College Life, packed with 21 fun-filled, informative chapters, great illustrations and more!

Name _____ Signature _____
Address _____
City _____ State _____ Zip _____
High School _____ College _____

KNUTHOUSE
215 Godwin Avenue
Midland Park, NJ 07432

PROBLEM AT OUR END IS, KIDS IN HIGHSCHOOL AREN'T THINKING ABOUT
COLLEGE ADJUSTMENT, MUCH AS THEY SHOULD BE.

                                                    -GUIDANCE DIRECTOR, W HS

I was really impressed with some of your insight concerning
college. You have a smooth, pleasure-to-read style of writing
that makes one feel as though he is right in the room talking
to you. (Thank God I'm not though cuz your room was a pig sty.)

                                    -S."Longdong" C., pre-med student,
                                      resident advisor, lousy drummer

It tells the down truth of it-- What to expect so you don't go in
scared.
                                    -C.V., Economics major, S College

When I read the book the second time I realized that the closer
I get to senior year, the more the logic falls into place.
I really didn't notice the first section on friends on my initial
reading, but this reading it struck home. I'm betting that each
reading will allow me to discover another section.

                                    -J.P., psychology major, wide receiver,
                                      sun god, Osmond brother

...cozy...warm... makes you feel as if you're not alone.
A few idiots may take some things the wrong way, but it's
true- it's real.
                                    -M.G., commuter, F University

It's right there- funny and accurate. He's not encouraging
bad study habits, just making light of some of the pressure.

                         -D.B., English & Economics major, University of R,
                            Wall Street tycoon, runs me all over the court

You should learn as much about yourself and others as you can--
college is a perfect opportunity. Sure, you're going to work
hard, but why not take advantage of the times when you're not
studying to learn in a less regimented way? Many of the concepts
in this book can be applied to personnel management, recruitment,
and leadership.
                              -G.B., Biology major, University of T,
                                sorority member

I like your analogies... I hope it all comes through for you as
it is much deserved.
                             -B.C., Management Trainee, life saver,
                             no more gut

When I went to college, I had that stereotype of college:
Professors are Gods, thirst for knowledge, and in general a
serious attitude about learning. When I graduated it was
far from it. My attitude had changed. Getting an A was no
longer a major priority. Friendships and athletics started
to play a larger role in my life. And I'm not saying I threw
in the towel or turned into a bar room waste product, but
relationships were contributing more to my learning experience
than books.
    In retrospect, being out in the business world now and
applying things in a practical way, I have this last comment:
If books were the only part of my maturation, I'd be an
insensitive, senseless machine.

                                            -R.D., Chemical Engineer

Good luck in reaping the benefits of your labor-
the book proved to be quite enjoyable.

                            -Director of Student Life,
                              V University

The vulgar reference in chapter X seems wholly unnecessary
and only detracts from an otherwise worthy piece of writing.
It might be a good thing to have a copy around.

                        -memo from junior Electrical Engineering
                         student C University to Guidance
                         Director P HS

I read over your book again a few weeks ago, and it was the best
thing I could have done because it made me feel really good about
college. I really appreciate it when someone expresses themselves
well, especially when it comes to things I've put a lot of thought
into myself.

                        -E.C., Mechanical Engineer, recent
                         graduate, relocates every
                         other day, removes nail polish
                         with a bunson burner

Brings out a lot of information that you wouldn't ordinarily
be able to obtain... Kids shouldn't panic over schoolwork.
Take part in as much as you can.

                        -D.A., Accounting Major, R University,
                         CPA, too nice a guy to abuse

...masterpiece... optimistic... generalities- I would have
liked to have seen more specifics. It's all relative, though.

                        -D.D., Law student, never loses
                         at cards, still has a gut

Its a cute book, and I love the quotes-- you have an especially good
collection.

                        -M.L.T., College Freshman

I am returning your book "Four Years." I was not pleased with it
at all. Don't try sending me another bill because I'm not giving
you a dime for that piece of CRAP!

                        -C.D., college freshman,
                         unsatisfied customer

Thanks for sending FOUR YEARS. I think if you could get a HS senior
to read a book, IT WOULD REALLY SELL! Same for college freshmen.

                        -MJR, Literary Agent

It should benefit mankind.

                        -T."Balls" E., conservative liberal, became
                         liberal conservative, soccer
                         star, IQ of two people, leaving
                         liver to science

...It breaks the ice. I've seen similar books that are so serious and
dull. This book is really funny- it eases the tension about going to
college. I read it cover to cover.

                        -M.(don't know last name), Junior,
                         R College, communications major

FOUR YEARS has come out well- all of a piece and forceful. Early in the semester my impression was unfavorable because of the jazzy tone. Now my attitude has changed. You speak in a distinctive voice. Tone, suprisingly, is broad in range, from humorous to sentimental. The result is powerful.

-Professor RWB

Very funny, accurate and helpful. The balance between people and book knowledge is important. You should do your work and enjoy other things, too. Reads easily... Extremely enjoyable and recommendable.

-N.K., Chemistry major, M College; registered nurse, clinical researcher

Don't lose your delightful sense of humor; one needs it to survive life on this planet.

-Guidance Director, I HS

...Makes a lot of valid points, especially concerning adjustment to college. It takes a while.

-Jake B., Engineer, football team, CAPTAIN, soulman

Loved FOUR YEARS! Would you please send another?

-M.P., Librarian; Concord, NH Highschool

Dear Sir,
 Find enclosed a check for the book. I thought it was enlightening and entertaining. (I had more to say about the book but I didn't want the author [whoever it (sic) is] to get a swelled head) Thank you.

-G.Z., HS student

Sorry I'm late. You know how us college students are about paying bills. ...By the way the book was excellent.

-E.B., college freshman, account deliquent

I enjoyed Four Years very much.

-B.F., college freshman

Reading his accounts of college, one can not help but smile; he brings back warm and pleasant memories. More to the point, his advice is very much on target. He writes as one who is in touch with college life as well as in touch with himself.
 The "Knucklehead's Guide" is full of warmth and wit and wisdom. I recommend it for parents who are concerned about their children's college experience. Most of all, however, I recommend it for those young people who want to know what college is like and need some practical advice on how to enjoy and profit from the four years.

-Guidance Director, R HS

You'll probably get as many different opinions as there are guidance counselors. Stick with your convictions- always.
 Will HS seniors appreciate your book now? Or will they learn better as college freshmen? I think the latter. Get more opinions from students.

 Good Luck!

-D.S., publishing and design consultant, author and lecturer, grandfather of two college students

I was very impressed with your book, because I really feel you touched on some of the most important aspects of college life. I most definately agree that the relationships you develop in college are the most important aspect of your four years. In the business world, being able to communicate with, and understand others is seventy percent of the game. You do need to know the technical side, but what you haven't learned they can teach you. It's a lot harder to teach someone to communicate than it is to teach them theory.

I also feel the stress you placed on getting to know and understand your teachers is very important. (Hard to do at a large school, but one of the major advantages of a small school). Your instructors are usually very knowledgeable and eager to help in many areas besides class work.

Very readable, informative as well as humorous book.

> -A.G., Business major, now with Touche Ross & Co.

Some book.
> -J."Moose"K., money printer, hoop stand out, stunt man, flasher, still owes me $10

Before I went to college I was terrified because I had no idea what lurked behind the huge tuition bill... I set off with a bunch of misconceptions that only "sophomore syndrome" and poor grades could shatter.

Sure college was a great time, but it contained some "rough" times, too. If I had read this book <u>before</u> I went to college, I would have been better prepared, enlightened and grateful I had. I know this book was written with much thought and sensitivity-- and it's a riot, too!

> -K.F., psychology major, F College, Masters Degree in counseling, social worker

Everything isn't etched in stone... Some people adopt the attitude that they're dropping out of society for four years- It shouldn't be this big gap. You don't sit around preparing for life-
It's here now. Do some work outside of college; try things in a practical setting.

College isn't a torture zone- Some kids come out of highschool as straight A students and fall apart if they get a C in Chem 1. C is average-- it's not failure.

...I could spend an extra 25 hours a week on a course and burn my eyes out, but it's overkill. If your head needs that, fine, but I'd rather see that time being spent on practical application.

Also, college doesn't guarantee you a job-- just an education. How far you take it depends on the individual.

> -A.M., 800 SAT Math, 730 Verbal, Chemistry major, D University, ex-grease pit waitress, aspiring bassist

I won't lie to you- I didn't read your whole book, just a little more than half. But I found it to be straightforward, insightful, witty, accurate, and generally enjoyable. It's obvious that the "best writer in the house" has a great talent at getting truthful points across in a uniquely humorous style. Now if that same author would only get a personality and a future, he'd be set. I always heard that the best writers are (unprintable).

> -Fred. P., economics major, fraternity president, social deviate